Insights

General Editor: Clive Bloom, Princi
  Middlesex Polytechnic
Editorial Board: Clive Bloom, Brian
  Lesley Bloom and Hazel Day

Insights brings to academics, students and general readers the very
best contemporary criticism on neglected literary and cultural areas.
It consists of anthologies, each containing original contributions by
advanced scholars and experts. Each contribution concentrates on a
study of a particular work, author or genre in its artistic, historical
and cultural context.

Published titles

Clive Bloom (*editor*)
JACOBEAN POETRY AND PROSE: Rhetoric, Representation and
  the Popular Imagination
TWENTIETH-CENTURY SUSPENSE: The Thriller Comes of Age
SPY THRILLERS: From Buchan to le Carré

Clive Bloom, Brian Docherty, Jane Gibb and Keith Shand (*editors*)
NINETEENTH-CENTURY SUSPENSE: From Poe to Conan Doyle

Dennis Butts (*editor*)
STORIES AND SOCIETY: Children's Literature in its Social
  Context

Gary Day (*editor*)
READINGS IN POPULAR CULTURE: Trivial Pursuits?

Gary Day and Clive Bloom (*editors*)
PERSPECTIVES ON PORNOGRAPHY: Sexuality in Film and
  Literature

Brian Docherty (*editors*)
AMERICAN CRIME FICTION: Studies in the Genre
AMERICAN HORROR FICTION: From Brockden Brown to
  Stephen King

Rhys Garnett and R.J. Ellis (*editors*)
SCIENCE FICTION ROOTS AND BRANCHES: Contemporary
  Critical Approaches

Robert Giddings (*editor*)
LITERATURE AND IMPERIALISM

Robert Giddings, Keith Selby and Chris Wensley
SCREENING THE NOVEL: The Theory and Practice of Literary
  Dramatization

Graham Holderness (*editor*)
THE POLITICS OF THEATRE AND DRAMA

Paul Hyland and Neil Sammells (*editors*)
IRISH WRITING: Exile and Subversion

Maxim Jakubowsi and Edward James (*editors*)
THE PROFESSION OF SCIENCE FICTION

Mark Lilly (*editor*)
LESBIAN AND GAY WRITING: An Anthology of Critical Essays

Christopher Mulvey and John Simons (*editors*)
NEW YORK: City as Text

Adrian Page (*editor*)
THE DEATH OF THE PLAYWRIGHT? Modern British Drama and
  Literary Theory

Frank Pearce and Michael Woodiwiss (*editors*)
GLOBAL CRIME CONNECTIONS: DYNAMICS AND CONTROL

John Simons (*editor*)
FROM MEDIEVAL TO MEDIEVALISM

Jeffrey Walsh and James Aulich (*editors*)
VIETNAM IMAGES: War and Representation

Gina Wisker (*editor*)
BLACK WOMEN'S WRITING

Further titles in preparation

Stories and Society

Children's Literature in its Social Context

Edited by

Dennis Butts

MACMILLAN

First published 1992 by
MACMILLAN ACADEMIC AND PROFESSIONAL LTD
Houndmills, Basingstoke, Hampshire RG21 2XS
and London
Companies and representatives
throughout the world

ISBN 0–333–52246–X hardcover
ISBN 0–333–52247–8 paperback

A catalogue record for this book is available
from the British Library.

Printed in Hong Kong

For Mary with love

Contents

Notes on the Contributors

Gillian Avery is the author of many children's books and won the *Guardian* award for children's fiction for *A Likely Lad* in 1971. Her critical books include *Nineteenth Century Children* (1965) and *Childhood's Pattern* (1975), and she is currently working on a history of American Children's Literature.

Dennis Butts teaches on the MA course on Children's Literature at Reading University, and is Chairman of the Children's Books History Society. He has written widely on various aspects of nineteenth-century literature and children's books, and edited Frances Hodgson Burnett's *The Secret Garden* and H. Rider Haggard's *King Solomon's Mines* in the World's Classics series for Oxford University Press.

Peter Hunt is a Senior Lecturer in English and Communications at the University of Cardiff, and he is the author of children's books, such as *A Step Off the Map* (1985). He has recently edited *Children's Literature: The Development of Criticism* (1990).

Fred Inglis is Reader in Education at Warwick University. An active journalist and broadcaster, he has been a Parliamentary candidate four times, and his publications include *The Promise of Happiness* (1981) and *The Management of Ignorance* (1985).

Elizabeth Keyser teaches American Literature at Hollins College, in Roanoke, Virginia. She has published essays on Frances Hodgson Burnett and other American women writers, and is completing a book-length study of Louisa May Alcott's fiction.

Perry Nodelman is a Professor of English in the Department of English in the University of Winnipeg. A former President of the Children's Literature Association of America, Professor Nodelman is completing a book about how children's picture books tell stories.

Jeffrey Richards is Professor of Cultural History at Lancaster University. A broadcaster and historian of popular culture, his publications include *The Age of the Dream Palace* (1984) and *Happiest Days: The*

Public Schools in English Fiction (1988). He recently edited *Imperialism and Juvenile Literature* (1989).

Charles Sullivan III is a Professor and Director of Graduate Studies in the English Department at East Carolina University, where he teaches American Folklore and North European Mythology. He is the author of *Welsh Celtic Myth and Modern European Fantasy*, and the editor of the *Children's Folklore Review*. His articles on mythology, folklore, fantasy and science fiction have appeared in a variety of journals and anthologies.

Mark I. West is an Associate Professor at the University of North Carolina at Charlotte, North Carolina, and editor of *Before Oz: Juvenile Fantasy Stories from Nineteenth-Century America* (1989).

Introduction

DENNIS BUTTS

Children's literature did not suddenly appear as if by magic. It came into existence in printed form in the eighteenth century, though religious and instructional books had appeared earlier, and grew to fruition in Britain and America in the nineteenth century because of quite specific developments in society. The ideas of such men as John Locke (1632–1704) and Jean-Jacques Rousseau (1712–78) helped to change European perspectives on the nature of childhood, and to suggest that it had needs and values of its own; and their ideas were enriched and extended by the Romantic Revival and the works of such writers as Blake, Wordsworth and Dickens. The gradual spread of education from the latter half of the eighteenth century onwards, first through the Sunday School Movement, and then through the faltering steps towards providing state education, meant that more children learned to read. And finally innovations in printing and publishing meant that it became possible to produce attractive books more cheaply for children. The combination of these several forces was irresistible, and throughout the nineteenth century more and more books were published for children.[1]

As in many societies, however, the interests, concerns and values of that society's dominant class pervaded its literature, including its children's books. Even so apparently light-hearted a publication as John Newbery's *A Little Pretty Pocket-Book* (London, 1744), despite its rhymes and woodcuts of children at play, reveals the influence of mercantile values and the Protestant Work Ethic, in its 'Letter from Jack the Giant-Killer,' and its promise of material rewards for being virtuous. Similarly the Evangelical Movement, with its genuine Christian faith and equally genuine desire to uphold most of the *status quo* deeply affected many children's stories at the end of the eighteenth and beginning of the nineteenth century. Hannah More's *The Shepherd of Salisbury Plain* (Bath and London, 1795), the tale of a poor but contented countryman without any wish for social change, is one of many examples.[2]

But as children's literature itself evolved in response to certain broad movements in society, so within the field of children's literature various sub-genres emerged in response to more particular historical developments. The Adventure Story, for example, can be seen at least in part as a reflection of British imperialism in the nineteenth century, as such tales as G. A. Henty's *With Clive in India: or the Beginnings of an Empire* (London, 1884) make clear, and the popularity of Henty's books in America, shown by the publication of so many official and pirated editions, suggests that their ideological and narrative appeal extended well beyond narrow national frontiers. Indeed the enduring popularity of the adventure story in the twentieth century by such authors as Rosemary Sutcliff and Robert Westall suggests that the form is still able to reflect some of society's dominant concerns, although these are related more to questions of identity and of survival, and to the ecological and cultural dangers that threaten in the closing decades of the twentieth century rather than to imperial expansion.

Similarly the rise of the School Story, with the publication of such books as *Tom Brown's Schooldays* (London, 1857), can be seen as an expression not only of changing attitudes towards childhood and adolescence, and the spread of education in general, but to the development of the reformed public (i. e. private) schools in England from the middle of the nineteenth century. Later school stories in their turn have responded to further changes in society and in education, and works produced since World War II, such as Robert Cormier's *The Chocolate War* (New York, 1974) or BBC-TV's *Grange Hill* (1977 onwards), have reflected not only the changing mores of modern schools but the challenges and pressures of post-industrial society as a whole.

Equally, it can be argued that the changing size and character of the family household in the late eighteenth and early nineteenth century contributed to the emergence and evolution of the Family Story. Early didactic tales, such as Maria Edgeworth's *The Parent's Assistant* (second edition, London, 1796) and Mrs Sherwood's *The History of the Fairchild Family* (Part I, London, 1818), reflect the patriarchal values of the time as unquestionable social norms, but later stories, such as Charlotte M. Yonge's *The Daisy Chain* (London, 1856) and Louisa M. Alcott's *Little Women* (Boston, 1868), as well as revealing cultural differences between family life on opposite sides of the Atlantic, either consciously or unconsciously, begin to offer more complex views of family relationships. It is not surprising to find the even more radical changes taking place in twentieth-century family life being revealed in contemporary novels by such writers as Betsy Byars and Janni Howker.[3]

Children read books for their stories, however, to find out what happens next, and for many children the most potent form of story-telling they experience in their early childhood is the folk or fairy tale, with its identifiable hero or heroine, and its familiar patterning of narrative events, such as the loss of parents, the acquisition of a faithful companion, an educational initiation, a quest, and a triumphant conclusion. The sophisticated *written* stories of the nineteenth century were not folk tales, of course, but the new sub-genres of children's stories soon established their own modes and conventions, often because of the decisive role individuals such as Captain Marryat or Thomas Hughes played in their origination. In *Tom Brown's Schooldays*, for example, Hughes established a narrative sequence, describing the young schoolboy's home, his initiation into various school rites, and the development and complication of relationships culminating in a great sporting or academic triumph, which has influenced almost all school stories ever since. Investigations of a genre's modes and conventions may often reveal a formulaic approach, which many readers found reassuring, but also expose a good deal about a society's values and attitudes. Studies of a sub-genre of children's literature may disclose, for instance, not only the way a society operates, but the way it would like to be perceived operating. British adventure stories nearly always see British imperialism as completely fair and altruistic, to give an obvious example. Investigations of the constituents of, and assumptions behind the nineteenth-century Family Story nearly always reveal the gender stereotyping characteristic of much British and American society in this period.

Studies of a story's structure, furthermore, may not only reveal the way a writer uses traditional narrative elements, which reassure the reader psychologically that he or she is on familiar ground – a very important point for young children who may be struggling to 'read' a narrative – but also show how a writer may vary the traditional elements to make unexpected points and to give variety. Mrs Hodgson Burnett's *The Secret Garden* (London, 1911), for example, employs the very familiar pattern of a *Cinderella*-type narrative, in the story of the lonely and neglected heroine Mary Lennox, but varies the expected formula by depicting the young heroine as not merely neglected but also erratically spoiled and petulant, and this makes Mary's growth and final triumph even more remarkable.

Sometimes, indeed, the narrative conventions by which genres have been traditionally structured are subverted in a way which may help the reader to see how a writer or a writer's society handle or even conceal a problem within that society. In many realistic stories of hardship and poverty, success comes to the hero or heroine at the end, not simply through the industry and piety recommended by the author, but through the unexpected intervention of a 'Fairy Godmother', in the person of a wealthy and philanthropic outsider. In *Enoch Roden's Training* (London, 1865) by Hesba Stretton, for example, the financial problems which threaten to ruin the Roden family are resolved by the discovery of a previously unheard-of rich uncle. Thus a *realistic* story's reversion to a *romantic* story's formula at a critical moment may expose an unselfconscious awareness of a society's difficulties.[4]

Many of the essays in this collection are essentially discussions of genre, examining such forms as the Adventure Story, the School Story, the Family Story, and Fantasy, so that the reader can see how different genres developed their own sets of rules, often in response to quite specific social, historical and cultural situations. The ways social changes can affect the development of genres is also illustrated by the comparative nature of the essays which often consider both early and later examples of a genre, and look at the way the changing context may have affected the form. In the essay on the Adventure Story, for example, nineteenth-century works by such authors as G. A. Henty, with their self-confident treatment of imperialism and 'pluck' or manliness, are compared with modern adventure stories by such writers as Monica Hughes and Robert Westall, with their reflection of more troubled, late twentieth-century values.

But children's literature is not simply a reflection of such conditioning factors as its age's ideology or the circumstances of publishing at a particular time. To see literature as a straightforward response to social conditions is too deterministic and reductive. Literary creation is a process in which the writer often struggles with the world he or she sets out to depict, so that while some works undoubtedly do reflect their society in very passive ways, others articulate its contradictions, question its values, or even argue against them. Far from endorsing the nineteenth-century stereotyping of children, especially girls, as over-dependent on adults, for example, Mrs Ewing's stories, such as *Mary's Meadow* (London, 1884), often depict children acting independently, and frequently make fun of adult behaviour. Fantasy often surprises conventional expectations, too. E. Nesbit's *The Story of the Amulet* (London, 1906), for example, which is apparently an escapist story about a sand-fairy, a group of middle-class children

xiv   *Dennis Butts*

and time-travel, actually voices serious concerns about society, when
the Queen of Babylon, on an unexpected visit to Edwardian London,
comments on the state of the poor inhabitants of the Mile End Road.

> And now from the window of a four-wheeled coach the Queen
> of Babylon beheld the wonders of London. Buckingham Palace
> she thought uninteresting; Westminster Abbey and the Houses of
> Parliament were little better. But she like the Tower, and the river,
> and the ships filled her with wonder and delight.
> 'But how badly you keep your slaves. How wretched and poor
> and neglected they seem,' she said, as the cab rattled along the
> Mile End Road.
> 'They aren't slaves; they're working-people.' said Jane.
> 'Of course they're working-people. That's what slaves are. Don't
> you tell me. Do you suppose I don't know a slave's face when I see
> it? Why don't their masters see that they're better fed and better
> clothed? Tell me in three words.'
> No one answered. The wage-system of modern England is a
> little difficult to explain in three words even if you understand it
> – which the children didn't.
> 'You'll have a revolt of your slaves if you're not careful,' said the
> Queen.
> 'Oh no,' said Cyril; 'you see they have votes – that makes them
> safe not to revolt. It makes all the difference. Father told me so.'
> 'What is this vote?' asked the Queen. 'Is it a charm? What do
> they do with it?'
> 'I don't know,' said the harassed Cyril; 'it's just a vote, that's all!
> They don't do anything particular with it.'
> 'I see,' said the Queen; 'a sort of plaything.'[5]

Each essay which examines a genre in this collection is followed
by discussion of a particular text or author in order to see how a
more detailed analysis of specific works relates not only to the
generic conventions behind them, but also the ways in which
individual writers or works reflect, argue with, or even subvert the
ideologies of the society in which that work was produced.

Jeffrey Richards's essay associates the rise of the School Story with
social and educational events in the nineteenth century, especially
the impact of Dr Arnold on Rugby School, and examines the evolution
of the form in relation to the philosophy of athleticism later in the
century. As well as defining the format of the School Story, and its

appeal, especially to working-class readers, Jeffrey Richards discusses the emergence of day-school stories in the second half of the twentieth century, and, recognising the fact that for many children fiction is no longer confined to books, concludes with a discussion of BBC Television's popular school series *Grange Hill*. Perry Nodelman's discussion of Robert Cormier's *The Chocolate War* and *Beyond the Chocolate War* links two modern American school stories to the tradition of *Tom Brown's Schooldays*, but, through a detailed analysis of Cormier's narrative techniques, shows how books produced within an apparently limited genre are capable of sustaining themes of violence and guilt.

Gillian Avery's essay on 'Home and Family: English and American Ideals in the Nineteenth Century' very firmly relates the differences between the behaviour of English and American children in the nineteenth-century Family Story to the cultural and social differences between Britain and the United States, especially the complex Victorian class system, which deeply affected such writers as Mrs Molesworth, when contrasted with the more robust 'pioneering' tradition of America, which influenced such writers as Jacob Abbott. Elizabeth Keyser's discussion of *Little Women*, however, shows how Louisa M. Alcott articulated the constraints and disappointments of conventional (male-oriented) family life in America in a novel which actually threatens to subvert many of the assumptions which lay behind family life, and not only in America.

Dennis Butts's essay on the Adventure Story relates the rise of the form in the nineteenth century not only to the literary models of Defoe and Scott but to the emerging ideology of British imperialism, but his essay also attempts to show how an artist such as R. L. Stevenson could exploit the form for delicate moral effects, and that modern adventure stories increasingly reflect the values of themes of a post-imperialist society. Fred Inglis pursues this theme, and, arguing the post-1914 collapse of traditional 'heroic' values and more recent decline of socialism, suggests that the novels of Jan Needle, especially his historical sea-story *A Fine Boy for Killing* (London, 1979), reflect these changes and attempt to articulate some kind of political reconciliation.

Charles Sullivan's essay on Fantasy attempts to define this elusive genre and traces its origins to the crucial influences of *Frankenstein*, (London, 1818), *The Water Babies* (London, 1863), *The Princess and the Goblin* (London, 1872) and William Morris's *The Wood Beyond the World* (London, 1894). After describing various sub-divisions of the genre,

Dr Sullivan concludes by suggesting that J. R. R. Tolkein's works of High Fantasy, far from being escapist literature, reflect the pressures and problems of the modern world. Peter Hunt's discussion of *Winnie-the-Pooh* offers a detailed analysis of a work of Domestic Fantasy, in a way which brings out the ambiguities of A. A. Milne's stories. Finally, Mark West's comparison of the film-version of *The Wizard of Oz* (1939) with Frank Baum's original book of 1900, as well as reminding us again of the popularity and impact of non-print fiction, serves to illustrate how a story which originally challenged prevailing notions of femininity, became a film which reflected the more conventional notions of female behaviour prevalent in American society in the late 1930s.

NOTES

1.   For the history of British children's books, see especially B. Alderson (ed.), F. J. Harvey Darton, *Children's Books in England: Five Centuries of Social Life*, third edition revised (Cambridge: Cambridge University Press, 1982). For an account of the influence of Locke and of Rousseau, see Peter Coveney, *The Image of Childhood: The Individual and Society: a Study of the Theme in English Literature*, revised edition with an introduction by F. R. Leavis (Penguin, Harmondsworth, 1967). For information about the connections between education, publishing and children's reading, see R. D. Altick, *The English Common Reader*, (Chicago: University of Chicago Press, 1957). For information about changing perceptions of childhood and children's literature in America, see, *inter alia*, Joseph M. Hawes and N. Ray Hiner (eds). *American Childhood: A Research Guide and Historical Handbook*, (Westport, Conn.: Greenwood, 1985).
2.   See, for example, Geoffrey Summerfield, *Fantasy and Reason: Children's Literature in the Eighteenth Century*, (London: Methuen, 1984), pp. 81–6. Among many studies of Evangelical writing, see Margaret Nancy Cutt, *Ministering Angels; a Study of Nineteenth-Century Evangelical Writing for Children*, (Wormley: Five Owls, 1979).
3.   See Betsy Byars, *The Animal, The Vegetable and John D. Jones*, (London: Bodley Head, 1982) and *The Pinballs*, (London: Puffin, 1980): and Janni Howker, *The Nature of the Beast*, (London: Julia MacRae, 1985).
4.   See J. S. Bratton, *The Impact of Victorian Children's Fiction*, (London: Croom Helm, 1981), pp. 63–101.
5.   E. Nesbit, *The Story of the Amulet*, (London: T. Fisher Unwin, 1906), pp. 195–6.

1
The School Story
JEFFREY RICHARDS

Popular fiction is one of the ways in which society instructs its members in its prevailing mores and ideas, its dominant role models and legitimate aspirations. It both reflects popular attitudes, ideas and preconceptions and generates support for selected views and opinions. So it can act – sometimes simultaneously – as a form of social control, directing the popular will towards certain viewpoints and attributes deemed desirable by those controlling the production of popular fiction, and as a mirror of widely held popular views. There is a two-way reciprocal process at work between producers and consumers. The consumers by what they buy tell the producers what they want. The producers, aiming to maximise profit, dramatise what they perceive to be the dominant issues and ideas of the day.

Popular fiction is undeniably selective in what it chooses to show. It provides images of society, constructed of selected elements and aspects of real life, organised into a coherent pattern governed by a set of underlying presuppositions. The process of selection confers status on issues, individuals and institutions which regularly appear in a favourable light. It legitimises, glamourises and romanticises particular mindsets. Generic literature, relying as it does on the regular re-use of the same elements, characters and situations, functions as a ritual, cementing the ideas and beliefs of society, enforcing social norms and exposing social deviants. As Joan Rockwell has written: 'Fiction is a social product but it also "produces" society . . . It plays a large part in the socialization of infants, in the conduct of politics and in general gives symbols and models of life to the population, particularly in those less-easily defined areas such as norms, values and personal and inter-personal behaviour.[1]

This is nowhere more true than in the realm of the school story. School is and has been for over a hundred years a universal experience and it is not surprising then that when juvenile literature evolved as a distinctive branch of fiction in the mid-nineteenth century, it

should have inspired a specific genre.[2] Juvenile literature emerged
in response to three developments: the discovery of adolescence as a
distinctive phase in human life, technological advances facilitating
the mass production of books and the Forster Education Act (1870)
which established free elementary schools in Britain and paved the
way for compulsory universal education, signalling to enterprising
publishers the creation of a huge potential new market. The aim of
the new juvenile literature was both to entertain and to instruct, to
inculcate approved value systems and acceptable gender images, in
particular gentlemanliness for the boys and domesticity for the girls.[3]

The emergence of the school story can only be appreciated in the
context of the history of the public schools. For the remarkable fact is
that for a hundred years the school story genre was dominated by
the public school story, despite the fact that only about three per cent
of the population actually went to such schools. This to some extent
reflects the background and ideals of the writers and publishers of
the early school stories. But it also reflects the tremendous influence
of the founding father of the genre, Thomas Hughes, and his enormously significant *Tom Brown's Schooldays*.

Tom Brown's Schooldays was an important part of the educational
debate in the nineteenth century about the public schools and their
reform. The unreformed public schools of the eighteenth and early
nineteenth centuries were self-governing boy republics, tribal, tur-
bulent, brutal and often drunken.[4] The Evangelicals, who mounted a
wide-ranging, large-scale assault on the ills of nineteenth-century
society, aiming to secure its pacification and purification, successfully remodelled the public schools in their own image, with the
promotion of the doctrine of 'Godliness and Good Learning'.

The mid-Victorian period saw a remarkable breed of headmasters
taking the schools by the scruff of the neck and transforming them
into respectable institutions – Cotton of Marlborough, Thring of
Uppingham, Benson of Wellington, Percival of Clifton, Vaughan of
Harrow. The school took control of the boys' lives in a way unthinkable in the days of the unreformed public schools. Uniforms were
introduced. Sport was promoted to use up the boys' surplus energies. Religion was advanced to the centre of school life, with compulsory chapel and the weekly sermon as the high point of moral
instruction. The prefects became the elite assistants of the headmaster. House and school loyalties were inculcated by competitive games,
school songs, school magazines and Old Boys' associations.[5]

The most celebrated exemplar of the change was Dr Thomas

Arnold, appointed headmaster of Rugby in 1828. Under his impact the English public school became uniquely among all western educational systems a place to train character. He was one of several heads who sought to apply the Evangelical influence to schools but he became the most famous because of the effect of two influential books by former Rugby pupils, Arthur Stanley's *Life and Correspondence of Dr Thomas Arnold* (1844) and Thomas Hughes's *Tom Brown's Schooldays* (1857).

Tom Brown is the most famous school story ever written, an autobiographical account of schooldays whose influence lay in its reflection, mythification and propagation of what was to become the dominant image of the public school, a place to train character and produce Christian gentlemen. It highlighted three classic themes: the socialisation of the schoolboy, the inculcation of manliness and the religious awakening. Over the years the third of these themes, so characteristic of the mid-Victorian period, was to diminish, but the other two were to remain constant factors of the boys' school story.

The book's ideological significance was threefold. It looked to the past, the present and the future. It recalled, recorded and mythified the Rugby of Dr Arnold, creating a selective image of Arnoldianism that was to be highly influential and was to eclipse the somewhat different reality. But onto his image of Arnoldianism, Hughes grafted other ideas dear to himself and not associated with Arnold especially: the ideals of Christian Socialism, Carlylean hero-worship and a strongly marked English nationalism.

The book is constructed in two halves: the first half of the story covers the arrival of Tom, the rough and tumble of school life, games-playing and character formation; the second half deals with Tom's religious awakening and his emergence as a Christian gentleman. It was Hughes's aim to propound a view of Christian manliness, or 'muscular Christianity' as it was sometimes called, which could counteract the brutal and drunken ethic of Regency manliness. But Hughes's book, which has remained continuously in print since 1857, and has been adapted for cinema and television, has existed on two levels of distortion. Arnold was equally interested in Christianity and education, opposed to fighting and not much interested in games. Hughes believed in fighting when necessary, and the importance of sport, and was not much interested in learning. His emphasis on these ideas in the book formed the view of Arnold that has survived in the popular consciousness: further testimony to the potency of popular fiction.

Aspects of Hughes's message fed into the games mania and Empire-worship of the later nineteenth century, eclipsing the pronounced religious element of the second half of the book which had been Hughes's avowed object in writing it in the first place. So just as he had given second place to the intellectual commitment of his old headmaster, Hughes's own religious priorities were downgraded by a later generation of readers in favour of sport and character-building.

Tom Brown's Schooldays founded the genre and was immediately followed in 1858 by another important work, *Eric*. It was written by Dean Farrar, one of the most influential churchmen of his day and later Master of Marlborough. Although it is probably the single most disparaged book in the history of juvenile literature and has been consistently compared unfavourably with *Tom Brown*, it was much read and was more influential than its critics have allowed. Admittedly the two books were written from different perspectives: *Tom Brown* from an Arnoldian background, *Eric* from a pre-Arnoldian. Hughes, optimistic, unintellectual and eternally boyish, wrote from the standpoint of the boy. He charted the triumphant evolution of a thoughtless, cheerful, healthy ordinary boy into a caring and committed Christian gentleman. Farrar, pessimistic, serious-minded, grave and intellectual, wrote from the standpoint of the schoolmaster. In a work conceived on the epic scale of Milton's *Paradise Lost*, which as a boy he had learned by heart, Farrar charted the gradual inevitable decline of a thoughtless, cheerful, healthy, ordinary English boy into a runaway and drunkard, seduced by his love of popularity and a too-easy-going nature. The two books complement each other perfectly and whatever the critics may say, Farrar painted an accurate picture of life in a pre-Arnoldian public school (King William's College, Isle of Man), accurately caught the psychology of some boys and reflected to the full the emotionalism that was part of the Evangelical temperament.[6]

Between them Hughes and Farrar set up themes, characters and archetypes that subsequent authors were to develop. But after *Tom Brown* and *Eric* there was a gap of some thirty years before the next major landmark. There were school stories by writers like the Revd T. S. Millington, the Revd H. C. Adams and Ethel Kenyon but their principal influence was Farrar rather than Hughes. They were set mainly in small private schools, rather than large public schools, were low on games and patriotism and high on moral didacticism. But none of them made the impact of *Tom Brown* and *Eric*.

The great leap forward came with the launching in 1879 of the

Boy's Own Paper, designed by the Religious Tract Society to counteract the 'pernicious influence' of the penny dreadfuls and attaining
by the end of the century a weekly print run of 665,000 copies, each
of which was believed to be read by two or three boys.[7] One of the
stars of the paper was Talbot Baines Reed, to whose school serials
the paper owned much of its early success. 'Very few people have
written schoolboy stories for schoolboys anything like so well' wrote
Harvey Darton.[8] In stories like *The Fifth Form at St. Dominic's*, *The
Willoughby Captains* and *Tom, Dick and Harry*, all issued in book form
after their initial appearance in the paper, Reed succeeded in fusing
the best elements of Hughes and Farrar but his moralising was
unobtrusive, his narrative vigorous and convincing and his boy
heroes instant identification figures for the young. Reed was un-
ashamedly writing moral fables but he was writing out of his own
experience about real boys and without the full weight of ideological
baggages that Hughes carried. Reed does not over-emphasise games,
for athleticism was not yet in full spate. Scholarships, the production
of the school magazine and friendships are as important as sport.
Reed endorses fagging, the prefectorial system and house loyalty.
Although he highlights certain characters, he is concerned to provide
a cross-section of school life and to see it in the round. The work of
Reed as a whole, although he rings the changes and maintain consistent freshness, liveliness and interest, does suggest that there is
truth in the complaint made by both Alec Waugh and P. G.
Wodehouse that the problem with schools is that nothing ever
happens.[9] Things do happen but within a restricted range of events
and recurrently, so that one tends to find that Reed's work is a
matter of themes and variations. Isabel Quigly has pointed out that
the plot of *St. Dominic's* shows how many of the incidents and patterns of events in Reed's stories became standard in the genre: 'The
stolen exam paper, the innocent wrongly accused, the suffering,
proud loneliness and final triumph, the boating accident, the runaway lost in the storm, rescued by the boy he had wronged and
brought back to the school half dead'.[10] They certainly recurred in
the work of Frank Richards, Reed's most illustrious successor. But
even before the great days of *The Magnet* a flock of school story
specialists – Hylton Cleaver, Richard Bird, Gunby Hadath, John G.
Rowe, Kent Carr, Harold Avery – writing both in periodicals and
books, endlessly reproduced, disseminated and perpetuated the
characters, incidents and ideology of Reed.

The outpouring of school stories in the last decades of the nine-

teenth century was part of what E. C. Mack called 'the greatest
upsurge of passionate adoration to which the schools had ever been
subjected', an upsurge manifested in memoirs, histories, poems and
songs which bathed the public schools in the glow of romance and
highlighted elements which were to become integral to the fiction:
friendships and floggings, japes and scrapes, customs and traditions.
Academic work was the significant exception.[11] E. C. Mack sum-
marised the standard school story format as it emerged at this time
and as it held until virtually the end of the public school genre:

> A boy enters school in some fear and trepidation, but usually with
> ambitions and schemes; suffers mildly or seriously at first from
> loneliness, the exactions of fag-masters, the discipline of masters
> and the regimentation of games; then he makes a few friends
> and leads for a year or so a joyful irresponsible and sometimes
> rebellious life, eventually learns duty, self-reliance, responsibility
> and loyalty as a prefect, qualities usually used to put down bullying
> or over-emphasis on athletic prowess; and finally leaves school
> with regret for a wide world, stamped with the seal of an institution
> which he has left and devoted to its welfare.[12]

Despite the formula, there were changes of emphasis. From the
1850s organised sports were a feature of the English public schools
but they were transformed into an obsession which bred an entire
philosophy – athleticism. The concepts of gentleman and sportsman
became interchangeable through the public schools and the revived
chivalry of the nineteenth century fed directly into the athleticism
cult. The word 'cult' is used advisedly for athleticism had its gods
and heroes, its hymns and rituals and was invested with the kind of
religious fervour that Arnold had sought to channel into Christian
commitment.

It was not Arnold but a coterie of celebrated mid-Victorian headmasters like Vaughan, Thring and Cotton who promoted games at
school. Organised games were introduced against a general background of vandalism and indiscipline as a potent means of social
control and character-formation. Sport was used to direct energy

and aggression into productive channels. It promoted manliness and
chivalry through the ideas of team spirit, leadership, loyalty, brav-
ery, fair play, modesty in victory and humility in defeat.

The triumph of athleticism is perfectly expressed in the school
stories of P. G. Wodehouse. Between 1902 and 1909 Wodehouse

published six public school novels and a collection of short stories and comic pieces about school. All had begun life a serials in boys' papers, principally *The Captain*. Several of the stories were set at Wrykyn which his old friend Bill Townend recognised as an idealisation of Wodehouse's beloved alma mater, Dulwich. The stories exalt the spirit and ethic of athleticism. Academic work plays little part in them. Sport is the measure of a boy and is totally dominant, as it had not been in *Eric, Tom Brown* or *St. Dominic's*. The stories are structured around vivid descriptions of cricket, rugby, boxing and athletics. The division between vice and virtue is absolutely clear: the rotters are bad sportsmen or non-sportsmen, smokers and sneaks, the heros are decent, clean-living sportsmen. Sport in Wodehouse takes on a moral dimension. It is central to school morale. It is used to help restore house order, *espirit de corps* and tone in *The Head of Kay's*, for instance. Sport makes a man of Sheen in *The White Feather*. The elements which in his important book *Athleticism in the Victorian and Edwardian Public School*, J. A. Mangan singles out as integral to athleticism are all to be found in Wodehouse: the prestigious house matches, the role of sporting house-masters, the colours system, the schoolboy sporting heroes, 'the bloods'.[13] By common consent *Mike* is Wodehouse's best school story but he was beginning to repeat himself, reworking elements from previous tales. But with the appearance of Psmith the story suddenly bursts into life and takes off with that distinctive Wodehousian love of wordplay, allusion, circumlocution, persiflage and banter. Psmith is Wodehouse Man fully formed and the authentic Wodehouse idiom is born as Wodehouse departs for good from the Victorian school for Edwardian clubland.

Three different stances towards the public school can be discerned across the full range of writing on the subject. The conformists accept and celebrate the system as it is. The reformers seek to retain the system with changes and modifications. The opponents seek to sweep the system away. The boys' school story was written on the whole by conformists. But among the reformers was one of the few undisputed geniuses to have contributed to the genre – Rudyard Kipling. *Stalky and Co.* (1899), inspired by Kipling's own schooldays at the United Services College, Westward Ho!, played a part in the debate about education provoked by Britain's failures in the Boer War. In his stories Kipling attacked the public school spirit of *Tom Brown* and the cult of athleticism, pouring scorn on the 'flannelled fools at the wicket and the muddied oafs at the goal' in his poem 'The Islanders'. The heroes of *Stalky and Co.* had not time for house spirit, school spirit, team spirit or organised games. They cheerfully break bounds, smoke, collaborate on their prep. But Kipling, in showing them engaging in a life of guerrilla warfare against the masters and the other boys, charts their acquisition of the initiative, courage, resourcefulness and self-discipline they will need to defend the Empire's frontiers. For Kipling recalled his schooldays through the filter of his subsequent experiences in India, his encounters with soldiers and district officers and his concern about the state of training for Imperial responsibility. Kipling also attacked the evangelical introspection and excessive piety of *Eric*, a source of permanent mockery for the Co. and the standard against which they gleefully measure their misdeeds. Nevertheless the trio's anarchy and rebelliousness is qualified by a strong sense of justice and retribution.

The classic oppositional text and the 'the first truly modern criticism of the public school by a major novelist'[14] is E. M. Forster's *The Longest Journey* (1907), in which the public school stands for a world of repression, loneliness and enforced conformity. *The Longest Journey* and Alec Waugh's *The Loom of Youth* (1917), which appeared oppositional at the time but can be seen in retrospect to have been merely reformist, represent a new development in public school fiction, the book for adults rather than for boys, though they were undoubtedly read by boys. Such novels began to appear at a time in the 1890s and the Edwardian Age of mounting criticism of the public schools from both ends of the political spectrum. It arose from concern based variously on charges of philistinism, amateurism, excessive conformity, class exclusivity and games worship. Within this adult market there were writers, working directly from their own experience, who were critical of the public schools (Forster and Waugh for instance) and who were warmly supportive (H. A. Vachell in *The Hill* and Ernest Raymond in *Tell England*). But it is important to stress here the divergence between high culture, generally hostile to the public schools, and popular culture, broadly supportive, which was to persist until well after World War II. Within the high culture there was a distinction between the reformers (Waugh) and the opponents (Forster). There had always been a current of criticism of the public school system and its product, but it peaked during and after world War I. Most 'serious' writers from the Great War onwards excoriated the public schools as hotbeds of homosexuality, brutality, snobbery and conformism. The system was seen as symbolic and symptomatic of the mindset which had caused the war. Lytton Strachey chose Dr Arnold as one of those Victorians eminently deserving debunking.

Graham Greene equated school, prison and factory as the means by which the capitalist system sought to suppress individualism and promote the uniformity it needs to survive and expand. Writers like George Orwell, Richard Aldington and E. M. Forster kept up the attack. W. H. Auden summed up the classic interwar response to the public schools when he wrote: 'At school I lived in a Fascist state'.[15]

But it is important to appreciate the extent to which such criticisms remained part of a narrow intellectual world, a world of high society salons and low circulation magazines, which rarely reached out to or affected the perceptions of the wider public. Of much greater significance in representing the attitudes of the general public to the public school in the interwar years were the middle-brow best-selling novels like *Tell England* and *Goodbye, Mr. Chips*, both of which reached far beyond the novel-reading public by their adaptation for the cinema, and the phenomenal success of Frank Richards's public school stories in the weekly boys' papers *The Magnet* and *The Gem*.

The work of Frank Richards represents the apotheosis of public school mythification. He stood in direct line of descent from Thomas Hughes, F. W. Farrar and Talbot Baines Reed. According to current estimates Richards wrote some 65 million words under 25 different pseudonyms between 1894, when his first stories were published, and Christmas Eve 1961 when he died. He created over one hundred fictional schools, of which the most famous were Greyfriars and St. Jim's. From 1907 to 1939 in *The Gem* and from 1908 to 1940 in *The Magnet* he provided a weekly 30,000 word story, as well as fulfilling commitments on other papers.[16]

Of all the schools Richards created, Greyfriars was closest to his heart and has been the most popular with readers. Greyfriars featured 'The Famous Five', Harry Wharton, Frank Nugent, Johnny Bull, Bob Cherry and Hurree Jamset Ram Singh, embryonic officers and gentlemen all and upholders of the public school code. Their comic counterpart and antithesis was Billy Bunter, whom Orwell called 'one of the best known figures in English fiction'.[17] He was the schoolboy Falstaff, a sacred monster, a larger than life embodiment of human failings, weaknesses and prejudices: fat, sly, idle, prevaricating, cowardly, snobbish, racist, greedy, vainglorious. His regular chastisement by beating, booting, bouncing, detention, suspension and exclusion confirms the need to check these weaknesses, to mortify the flesh and purify the spirit. The fact that he survives to offend again testifies to the enduring strength of human weakness. Their form-master and one of the most celebrated pedagogues in fiction

was the gimlet-eyed Henry Samuel Quelch. 'a beast but a just beast',
as the boys put it. When *The Magnet* closed in 1940, it looked as if the
world has seen the last of Bunter and Co. But after the war Frank
Richards revived them in hardback form and 33 titles eventually
appeared. Between 1952 ad 1961 BBC television ran five series of
Greyfriars adaptations, popular with adults and children alike.
Richards found himself in his seventies a national celebrity, with an
entry in *Who's Who*, regular newspaper and radio interviews and
when he died, an obituary in *The Times*. Even his death did not halt
the flow of stories. For in 1969 publisher Howard Baker launched a
series of facsimile reprints of the original *Magnets* which still continues, though purchased now almost exclusively by nostalgic adults
rather than by children.

The enduring appeal of these stories encapsulates something of
the attraction of the genre as a whole. First, there is the atmosphere
of timelessness, of comforting familiarity, of reassuring order, of
innocence. It is a world of unchanging patterns and eternal verities.
The Magnet followed the course of the school year precisely, with the
boys assembling in September for the autumn term. The boys played
football in the winter and cricket in the summer. There were Christmas
vacation stories and adventures in the summer holidays when the
boys generally undertook an expedition to some exotic clime – Brazil,
Egypt, India or the South Seas. One thing remained constant. The
boys always stayed the same age and each autumn as term began
and the cycle was initiated again, Harry Wharton and Co. were still
to be found in the Remove. It was this as much as anything which
ensured that feeling of timelessness. The elements of rituals and
repetition were important. As Gill Frith has written: 'The very formulaic and predictable nature of the school story, the experience of
knowing what's going to happen actively contributes to the enjoyment
of the reader, to the feel of being 'in control' of the reading process'.[18]

Second, there are the characters. Greyfriars featured a whole range
of rounded and convincing boy portraits. The idea that they are
stereotypes, which some later commentators have advanced, is quite
untenable. They are instead archetypes, something quite different. A
stereotype is a carbon copy of a well-established model; an archetype
is the creation of a definitive idealisation. There is irrefutable evidence
in the attitude of boy readers. The characters served as role models.
The historian Robert Roberts recalled that among his boyhood friends
in Edwardian Salford one, 'a natural athlete', modelled his conduct
on that of Harry Wharton and another adopted a jerky gait 'in his

attempts to imitate Bob Cherry's springy, athletic stride'. All his friends quite self-consciously incorporated Greyfriars slang into their own 'oath-sprinkled banter – 'Yarooh', 'My sainted aunt', 'Leggo' and a dozen others'.[19]

G. R. Samways, the *Magnet* sub-editor, recalled: 'To a great many readers these characters were not mere puppets of the author's creation but living, vital beings, leading a real existence in a real school'.[20] This is evidenced by the letter columns of the magazine, to which boys wrote seeking further information about the studies, habits, lives and backgrounds of the characters. The Amalgamated Press arranged with the GPO to have the many letters addressed to Greyfriars School delivered to them. The editors of *The Magnet* set great store by readers' letters, regarding them as a valuable indicator of the popularity of themes and characters.

The prime favourite was Bob Cherry, who according to Samways, 'had all the qualities which endeared him to youthful hearts – his sunny disposition, his gay courage, his sportsmanship, his irrepressible high spirits, and his ready championship of the underdog, all combined to make him not merely popular but universally beloved'. After Bob Cherry the most popular characters were Mark Linley and Herbert Vernon-Smith. Linley, a Lancashire factory boy who won a scholarship and thus achieved the hearts' desire of so many of *The Magnet*'s working-class readers, was a perfect role model for those readers, an exemplar of brains and hard work achieving success. Herbert Vernon-Smith, 'the Bounder of the Remove', reckless and defiant but basically honourable, was the boy who kicked over the traces but always proved true-blue in the end. Bunter, however, was not a role model and was 'an also ran in the popularity stakes': 'not many readers liked him' said Samways, 'a good many positively loathed him; yet he was a never-failing source of mirth and merriment to all'. Interestingly Harry Wharton, though he had his admirers, was not the top of the popularity poll. Samways explained: 'There was a touch of arrogance about him which caused him to be less well-liked than the characters already mentioned'.[21]

The third areas of appeal lies in the depiction of friendship. Friendship is central to the lives of children. Who is the best friend of whom, who is in whose gang, these are essential elements in the peer group dynamics of schoolchildren. The Famous Five are the ideal boy 'gang', a closely integrated group of friends, and if they fell out and the friendship was threatened, as it was periodically, the story struck home.

Fourthly there is the idealisation of school life, schooldays as they should be – japes and scrapes, soccer and cricket, study teas and practical jokes, and Dickensian Christmas hols. There were impots and whackings certainly but they were an accepted part of the system and life was fun. What Richards was at some pains to conceal was that he had himself never been to public school, which is perhaps why he chose to begin his autobiography when he was seventeen and had left school. As Mary Cadogan confirms, he attended a series of private day schools in Ealing and Chiswick.[22] It is significant that the chief critics of the stories have been former public schoolboys who have denounced the lack of authenticity. But this is irrelevant. He was writing in the main for boys who were not at and would never go to public schools. The power of the stories is that they are in one sense unreal. They are a distillation of elements of the public school story genre, transmuted into a dreamlike landscape, a mythic world, an alternative universe, whose surroundings and elements have a recognisable surface reality, but are subtly different, existing as it were out of time.

The stories for over fifty years dramatised and endorsed the public-school values and virtues, endorsing those characteristics which the British believed sustained their empire and justified their role as the world's policemen – team spirit and fairplay, duty and self-sacrifice, truth and justice. Richards believed firmly in discipline and the use of the cane and consistently denounced drinking, smoking and gambling. His attitude to women was one of chivalry. 'Never try to be unpleasantly witty on the subject of women – a subject that should be sacred to every self-respecting man' was his advice to aspiring writers.[23] He showed continual hostility to racism, snobbism and materialism. His inclusion of Hurree Jamset Ram Singh, the Nabob of Banipur, as one of the Co. was, he said, deliberate: 'By making an Indian boy a comrade on equal terms with English schoolboys, Frank felt that he was contributing his mite towards the unity of the Commonwealth and helping to rid the youthful mind of colour prejudice'.[24] His boys are patriotic, royalist and conservative, just like the bulk of the British people when Richards was writing.

Critics of Richards from George Orwell on have claimed that his stories lack sex and violence, any reference to war, poverty and social change and that his foreigners are cardboard characters.[25] The last charge is certainly true. There is no sex or violence and so much the better for that. World War I and the reality of poverty certainly do impinge on the stories very strongly. But then many of the critics of Richards have never read much of his work.

The readership of *The Magnet* and *The Gem* was drawn largely from the lower middle and upper working class. Perhaps the best assessment of the influence of the public school story upon them comes from Robert Roberts, one of the few historians to write from within the working class, in his moving account of Edwardian slum-life in Salford:

> Even before the first world war many youngsters in the working class had developed an addiction to Frank Richards' school stories. The standards of conduct observed by Harry Wharton and his friends at Greyfriars set social norms to which schoolboys and some young teenagers strove spasmodically to conform. Fights – ideally at least – took place according to Greyfriars rules: no striking of an opponent when he was down, no kicking, in fact, no weapon but the manly fist. Through the Old School we learned to admire guts, integrity, tradition; we derided the glutton, the American and the French. We looked with contempt upon the sneak and the thief. The Famous Five stood for us as young knights, *sans peur et sans reproche*. With nothing in our own school that called for love or allegiance, Greyfriars became for some of us our true Alma Mater, to whom we felt bound by a dreamlike loyalty . . . Over the years these simple tales conditioned the thought of a whole generation of boys. The public school ethos, distorted into myth, and sold among us weekly in penny numbers, for good or ill, set ideals and standards. This our own tutors, religious and secular, had signally failed to do. In the final estimate, it may well be found that Frank Richards during the first quarter of the twentieth century had more influence on the mind and outlook of young working class England than any other single person.[26]

What Roberts says of Richards can probably be applied generally to the genre of public school fiction.

There can be little doubt that public school fiction created for boys going to public school a fully formed picture of what to expect. According to Alec Waugh, preparatory school boys read Talbot Baines Reed assiduously in preparation for their translation to public school.[27] Many boys were to be disabused of their preconceptions on their arrival but others carried on reading public school stories in *The Captain* and *The Public School Magazine*, journals aimed specifically at a public school readership.

The largest audience for public school fiction, however, remained boys who had not been and would never go to public school. For them the image was a glamorous substitute for the often grim reality of their own schools, a wish-fulfilment of a particularly potent and beguiling kind. Writing of his childhood in Edwardian Battersea, Edward Ezard described his schooldays as 'lacking the public school glamour which made us avidly read *Magnet* and *Gem* week by week and swap them over until they became tatty indeed'.[28]

There has been much talk of World War I as a watershed but there was comparatively little change in the public school system in the interwar years. They remained institutions which sought to give their pupils moral training, to develop self-restraint, a proper sense of values and preparation of the exercise of power, whether as officers, administrators or statesmen. When World War II broke out there were more boys in independent schools than there had been in 1914, Edward C. Mack, writing in 1940, concluded: 'Though there was an attempt to modernize and eliminate evils, both the key ideas and the key practices of the Victorian schools remained intact, chiefly because Conservatives willed that they should. The post-war public school was still a class institution devoted to making leaders and statesmen out of privileged British youth'.[29] World War II was a much more significant watershed and afterwards the public schools began to achieve a more academic orientation with curriculum reform and the promotion of science. They became at last the centres of all-round academic excellence that Arnold and company had wanted. But they did so because the needs of the middle class had altered. The gradual dissolution of the empire and the reduction in size of the armed forces had meant that far fewer public school boys were needed as officers and administrators. Instead they were drawn to industry, finance and the city, and the old public schools necessarily had to change to meet these needs. But they have not done so against a background of a flourishing fictional genre. That petered out in the 1960s.

Exposure over a hundred years to a favourable cultural image of the public schools may well help to explain the surprising findings of a survey of British social attitudes in the early 1980s.[30] It revealed that 67 per cent of those questioned – and they covered both sexes, all ages and classes – favoured the retention of the public schools and only 19 per cent favoured their elimination or reduction. Even among Labour voters, only one in three favoured a reduction in the number of public schools and only one in five favoured abolition. This comes after twenty years of comprehensivisation with the Labour Party committed to the abolition of the public schools and with the schools often being depicted as symbols of a class-divided society. It can be seen as a tribute to the potency and staying power of Tom Brown, Mr Chips, Stalky and Co. and the Fifth Form at St. Dominic's.

Frank Richards's work was both the climax and the culmination of the public school story. He died on Christmas Eve 1961 and by 1972 Marcus Crouch was writing: 'The school story proper, that is one which does not look beyond the small, enclosed world of school, is dead . . . It was necessarily concerned with boarding school. Directly the little victims escaped home they became different beings. Writers, no longer drawn largely from the ranks of the public schools, were concerned with the everyday scene and with the experience of the majority of their readers. The complex pattern of school, home and the streets and fields offered wider opportunities than those afforded by classroom and dorm.'[31] But these opportunities were not grasped on a large scale until the 1960s and 1970s. Frank Richards's Bunter stories continued to appear until 1968 and Anthony Buckeridge's popular humorous preparatory school stories featuring Jennings and Darbishire ran from 1950 to 1977, their popularity enhanced by radio dramatisation as the Bunter stories were by television.

In 1948 Geoffrey Trease in his pioneering study of children's literature, *Tales Out of School*, was lamenting the almost total absence of day-school fiction: 'There is just as much potential drama and infinitely more scope for originality in depicting the life of any day-school. In an era like this, when we are trying to transform mere "school attendance" into that far richer thing "school life" a handful of good stories might help'.[32] He was writing in the context of the education debate stimulated by the Second World War which had produced the Butler Education Act (1944). This act raised the school leaving age to 15 and established a tripartite system of grammar, technical and secondary schools, leaving the public schools untouched.

Some writers sought to respond to the new situation by dramatising the grammar schools. Trease himself launched his five volume 'Bannermere' series in 1949.[33] They had a first person narrator, Bill Melbury, who attends a boys' grammar school at Winthwaite in the Lake District. Bill is uninterested in sport, ambitious to be a writer and part of a mixed-sex group of friends, which includes would-be detective Tim Darren and Penny Morchard, the Shakespeare-quoting, lame daughter of the local bookseller. Nevertheless the conflict between them and the local squire who in *No Boats on Bannermere* wants to ban them from the lake and its island echoes the running battle between the boys of Greyfriars and Sir Hilton Popper. There is undoubtedly more artistic and intellectual excitement than sporting interest in the stories. Bill develops his writing talent. Penny launches a troupe of travelling players, whose success persuades the old-fashioned headmaster of Winthwaite to permit joint drama productions between his boys and the girls of the County High School. Archaeological detective work is used to uncover a Viking treasure and intellectual ingenuity to decipher an eighteenth century coded diary. But, despite the presence of girls, there is no hint of romance between Bill and Penny until the very end of the final volume in the series, *The Gates of Bannerdale*, which covers their freshman year at Oxford. Until then they are merely chaste chums in a way that the more sophisticated and worldly characters of 1970s and 1980s school stories would not be.

However by general consent the most notable school stories of the 1950s were William Mayne's four books about the life of a choir school, a boarding school though of a particular kind, which began in 1955 with *A Swarm in May*. No great genre of grammar school fiction developed before the next major educational upheaval which in the 1970s resulted in the raising of the school leaving age to 16, the elimination of 11-plus selection, the compulsory imposition of a comprehensivisation and the abolition of many of the grammar schools. Although this was instituted in pursuit of an ethic of equal opportunity, in fact a new though informal tripartite system emerged consisting of public schools, well-resourced comprehensives and poorly-resourced comprehensives.

The secondary modern school had been even later than the grammar school in receiving mythification. E. W. Hildick made the key contribution here. Hildick, who taught at Dewsbury Secondary Modern in the early 1950s, declared: 'In my fiction for children I have always been compelled to give an accurate reflection of the contemporary background as I knew it'.[34] Between 1958 and 1963 Hildick produced seven novels featuring secondary modern schoolboy Jim Starling and his chums, 'The last Apple Gang'.[35] The setting is the inner city area Hildick was familiar with. Cement St Secondary Modern, Smogbury, 'a rambling, three decker, sooty-walled school' stands at the heart of a world of backstreets, waste ground, derelict factories and cheap caffs. His central characters are boys from rough backgrounds. But both teachers and pupils are recognisable human types: the boys sturdy, self-reliant, tough and humorous. The dialogue is convincingly demotic, apart from the necessary absence of profanity. The writing style is brisk, plain and naturalistic. The plots are simple and their keynote is humour. But the emphasis is on character, detail and incident and there is the clear intention of dignifying the experience of industrial working-class boys. In the opening story of the sequence, Jim and his friends clear Terry Todd of suspicion of slashing coats in the school cloak-room. Later, having formed themselves into a detective agency, they find a pensioner's lost dog, help a misunderstood Borstal boy on the run and round up a gang of ticket touts who fleece them on a trip to the Cup Final. In *Jim Starling and the Colonel*, Jim successfully refutes the disparaging comments on modern youth by a pompous Speech Day visitor by emulating the feats of the Victorian youth held up to them as an example. The idea of modern working-class youth proving itself as resourceful, self-reliant and deserving of respect as its earlier counterpart runs through several of the books, Like their public school counterparts, the boys still play sport, get into scrapes and pursue rivalries with other gangs and other schools. There is even a book devoted to a holiday in a haunted house, that much-used plotline of Frank Richards. What is different in Hildick's work is the setting and the dialogue rather than the actual content of the adventures.

But Hildick's books in their stance, setting and sympathies look forward to what is arguably the most significant and influential development in school fiction since *The Magnet*. Phil Redmond's BBC-TV series *Grange Hill* has run twice weekly in 16-week segments, with repeats, every year since 1977. There have been spin-off videos, tie-in paperbacks (a dozen or so to date) and annuals. It has also influenced other school fiction. There are some similarities than one would suspect between Greyfriars and Grange Hill. The two worlds have in common a multiplot structure, a large cast of characters, the intermingling of comedy and drama, and the recurrent and apparently timeless elements of school fiction – friendship and quarrels, japes and scrapes, sports and games, outings and rebellions. That old standby, the school ghost, has even appeared at Grange Hill. There are character types not that far removed from Greyfriars – heroes, bullies, bounders, japesters, entrepreneurs, sportsmen. Cheerful, goodnatured 'Ziggy' Greaves is *Grange Hill*'s equivalent of Bob Cherry, the reckless, quicktempered rebel 'Ant' Jones, the Herbert Vernon-Smith *de nos jours* and the diminutive delinquent 'Tegs', the latterday 'Flip', the Dickensian street waif and reformed criminal who turns up at Greyfriars. Just as Greyfriars had Bunter, so *Grange Hill* produced a cult figure in 'Tucker' Jenkins, an irrepressible and engaging Till Eulenspiegel, who when he left Grange Hill gained his own series *Tucker's Luck*, tracing his afterschool life.

But there are also significant differences. Some are obvious: Greyfriars was a public school, Grange Hill a comprehensive. Greyfriars was single-sex school; Grange Hill is mixed. At Greyfriars, the boys always remained the same age; at Grange Hill the pupils grow up and leave, so there are regular changes of cast. The day-school setting means an enhanced role for parents and families.

Perhaps the most significant difference is the presence of girls. Greyfriars, like Winthwaite Grammar and Cement St Secondary, was a boys' school. The mixed nature of Grange Hill, with equal space given to female characters as to male, means that the older denizens of the school are preoccupied with their love affairs, with pop music and with fashion in a way that would have been unthinkable for the boys of Greyfriars, for whom sport, japes, feasts in the dorm, outings and adventures were all-important. It has added a new character to the familiar cast of archetypes, the school 'heartthrob' ('Ant' Jones, Freddie Mainwaring, Robbie Wright). The programme has increasingly and explicitly highlighted an area totally absent from older school stories – sex. That reflects much wider changes in media, society and the image of adolescence. Story-lines have dramatised the sexual double standard towards pre-marital intercourse by boys and girls, a love affair between a female pupil and a young teacher, the cohabiting of a female pupil and her older, working boyfriend. Scenes in which girls discuss their periods or the virginity of their boyfriend have appeared. All this means that the programmer is moving closer to adult soaps like *Neighbours* and *EastEnders*, to the cast of which several of the actors from *Grange Hill* have graduated.

Secondly, the programme has made a point, like adult soap operas, of including social issues and over the years this has increased in proportion. They range from the immediate school problems of drug-taking, bullying, teenage drunkenness, dyslexia, the difficulties of the disabled and the prospects for female employment to wider social issues like homelessness, football hooliganism child abuse, racism, and animal rights campaigns. The programme has dealt movingly with the effects of grief at the death of a fellow pupil. The children are also shown developing social consciences as they continually engage in campaigns to raise money for the Third World, the underprivileged or the disabled.

Thirdly, *Grange Hill* has taken a consistent left-liberal stance on educational issues, promoting the idea of non-competitive sport, deriding the idea of a Latin school song, advocating pupil participation in school government and adopting a permissive attitude towards discipline. There has been less interest in academic learning than in personal fulfilment and interpersonal relations. But the fact that no one in the school shows any interest whatever in academic learning is perhaps taking things too far. There must be some children with intellectual interests, even in a comprehensive. With the poorest-educated population in the European Community, Britain might be seen to benefit from the dramatisation on television of the importance of learning. There is also the question of discipline. At Greyfriars, all the rags and stunts were conducted against a cheerfully accepted background of rules and authority, limits and retribution. The boys knew where they stood, how far they could go and what to expect if they crossed the boundaries. Despite the presence of a firm but fair headmistress in Mrs McCluskey, the situation is considerably vaguer at Grange Hill where no one seems to be punished for anything. One recent series resembled a running battle; with the ingenious and systematic persecution of a young male teacher, reduced to tears by his class; the tolerance, long beyond reason, of the disruptive presence of a semi-psychotic bully; and the wholesale flouting of school rules. There is too often an air of discourtesy and disorderliness, truculence and loutishness, with for instance pupils walking in and out of class during lessons with impunity. It is perhaps unfortunate under the circumstances that the only teacher to believe in strict discipline, the long-serving deputy head Maurice Bronson, is depicted as a neurotic martinet, permanently on the brink of apoplectic dementia. Unlike Henry Samuel Quelch, the revered form-master of the Greyfriars Remove, 'a beast but a just beast', Bronson was simply a beast. He has now been replaced by a new deputy head, a Filofax-wielding, economy-conscious, eager-beaver Thatcherite.

Grange Hill arguably exercises greater influence than *The Magnet* and *The Gem* because of the immediate visceral impact of television and the mode of naturalism in which it is conducted. It is less ritualistic and more documentary in nature than the Greyfriars stories. With its well-rounded characters, realistic setting, skilful

20 *Jeffrey Richards*

writing and adroit direction, it has established itself as an integral part of children's viewing. It has sought to exploit this by highlighting issues and themes it considers important and relevant. Its long-term effect on attitudes, views and perceptions has yet to be assessed.

NOTES

1. J. Rockwell, *Fact in Fiction: the Use of Literature in the Systematic Study of Society* (London, 1974), VIII, 4.

2. On the boys' school story see Isabel Quigly, *The Heirs of Tom Brown* (London, 1982); P. W. Musgrave, *From Brown to Bunter* (London, 1985); Jeffrey Richards, *Happiest Days: the Public Schools in English Fiction* (Manchester, 1988). Because of space constraints, this chapter has concentrated on the boys' school story, which originated first and set the pattern to which the later girls' school story initially conformed. On girls' school stories, see Mary Cadogan and Patricia Craig, *You're a Brick, Angela* (London, 1976), Kirsten Drotner, *English Children and Their Magazines 1751–1945* (New Haven and London, 1988); Gillian Freeman,*The Schoolgirl Ethic* (London, 1976) and Gill Frith, 'The Time of Your Life: the Meaning of the School Story' in Carolyn Steedman, Cathy Urwin and Valerie Walkerdine, eds, *Language, Gender and Childhood* (London, 1985), pp. 113–36.

3. On the development of juvenile literature for the mass market, see J. S. Bratton, *The Impact of Victorian Children's Fiction* (London, 1981) and Patrick Dunae, 'New Grub Street for Boys' in J. Richards, ed., *Imperialism and Juvenile Literature* (Manchester, 1989), pp. 12–33.

4. On this phase of the schools see J. Chandos, *Boys Together: English Public Schools 1800–1864* (London, 1984).

5. On the history of the reformed public schools see in particular J. Gathorne-Hardy, *The Public School Phenomenon* (Harmondsworth, 1975); J. R. de S. Honey, *Tom Brown's Universe* (London, 1977), T. W. Bamford, *The Rise of the Public School* (London, 1967); Rupert Wilkinson, *The Prefects* (London 1964); Ian Weinberg, *The English Public Schools* (New York, 1967); Brian Simon and I. Bradley, *The Victorian Public School* (Dublin, 1975); Edward C. Mack, *Public Schools and British Opinion 1780–1860* (London, 1938) and *Public Schools and British Opinion since 1860* (New York, 1940); and David Newsome, *Godliness and Good Learning* (London, 1961).

6. For a defence of *Eric* see Richards, *Happiest Days*, pp. 70–102; Patrick Scott, 'The School Novels of Dean Farrar', *British Journal of Educational Studies* 19 (1971), pp. 163–82; and Gillian Avery, *19th Century Children* (London, 1965), p. 146.

7. P. Dunae, *'Boy's Own Paper*: origins and editorial policies', *Private Library* 9 (1976), pp. 123–58.

8. F. J. Harvey Darton, *Children's Books in England* (Cambridge, 1982), p. 301.
9. P. G. Wodehouse, 'School Stories', *Public School Magazine* 8 (1901), p. 125; A. Waugh, *The Loom of Youth*, 1917 (London, 1929), p. 184.
10. Quigly, *Heirs of Tom Brown*, p. 83.
11. Mack, *Public Schools and British Opinion since 1860*, p. 134.
12. Ibid., pp. 201–2.
13. J. A. Mangan, *Athleticism in the Victorian and Edwardian Public School* (Cambridge, 1981).
14. John Reed, *Old School Ties*, (Syracuse, 1964), p. 135. Reed thoroughly surveys the hostile literature.
15. G. Greens, ed., *The Old School*, 1934 (Oxford, 1984), p. 9.
16. On Frank Richards and his work see Mary Cadogan, *Frank Richards: the Chap Behind the Chums* (London, 1988); W. O. G. Lofts and D. J. Adley, *The World of Frank Richards* (London, 1975) and E. Fayne and R. Jenkins, *A History of Gem and Magnet* (Maidstone, 1972).
17. G. Orwell, *Collected Essays, Journalism and Letters*, vol. I (Harmondsworth, 1970), p. 509.
18. G. Frith, 'The Time of Your Life', p. 118.
19. Robert Roberts, *The Classic Slum* (Harmondsworth, 1977), pp. 27, 160.
20. G. R. Samways, *The Road to Greyfriars* (London, 1984), p. 182.
21. Ibid., pp. 181–6.
22. Cadogan, *Frank Richards*, p. 12.
23. Ibid., p. 21.
24. F. Richards, *Autobiography* (London, 1965), p. 38.
25. The classic attack on *The Magnet* is in George Orwell's 'Boys' Weeklies', *Collected Essays, Journalism and Letters*, vol. I, pp. 505–31. Richards's reply is printed in the same volume, pp. 531–40.
26. Roberts, *Classic Slum*, p. 160–1.
27. A. Waugh, *Public School Life* (London, 1922), p. 31.
28. E. Ezard, *Battersea Boy* (London, 1979), p. 98.
29. Mack, *Public Schools and British Opinion since 1860*, p. 372.
30. R. Jowell and C. Airey, eds, *British Social Attitudes – the 1984 Report* (Aldershot, 1984), pp. 111–17.
31. Marcus Crouch, *The Nesbit Tradition: the Children's Novel in England 1945–1970* (London, 1972), p. 161.
32. G. Trease, *Tales Out of School* (London, 1948), p. 143.
33. The 'Bannermere' novels are: *No Boats on Bannermore* (1949), *Under Black Banner* (1950), *Black Banner Players* (1952), *Black Banner Abroad* (1953) and *The Gates of Bannerdale* (1957).
34. T. Chevalier, ed., *20th Century Children's Writers* (Chicago and London, 1989), p. 451.
35. The 'Jim Starling' novels are: *Jim Starling* (1958), *Jim Starling and the Agency* (1958), *Jim Starling and the Colonel* (1960), *Jim Starling's Holiday* (1960), *Jim Starling Takes Over* (1963), *Jim Starling and the Spotted Dog* (1963) and *Jim Starling Goes to Town* (1963).

2
Robert Cormier's
The Chocolate War:
Paranoia and Paradox

PERRY NODELMAN

'If schools are what they were in my time,' Tom Brown's father tells his son in *Tom Brown's Schooldays*, 'You'll see a great many cruel blackguard things done, and hear a great deal of foul bad talk.'[1] Robert Cormier's *The Chocolate War* suggests that, a century and a half later, schools are still what they once were. In this story of the evil machinations surrounding the fund-raising chocolate sale at Trinity High, the boys speak a great deal of foul bad talk, and do a great many cruel blackguard things; and that has created a lot of controversy. Many readers have complained that *The Chocolate War* is an inaccurate representation of reality, a vision of a hopeless world that encourages an unhealthy hopelessness in young readers.[2] During one of the many attempts to censor the book, in Proctor, Vermont in 1981, a parent nicely summed up this sort of response in two short sentences: 'I thought it was hostile and totally disgusting. To show that evil triumphs is kind of sick to me.'[3]

Sick or not, the ending of the novel is certainly unexpected – and a key factor in determining how readers respond to it. In refusing to take part in a chocolate sale in defiance of the powerful establishment of his school, Jerry Renault fits the pattern of the underdog non-conformist found frequently in fairy tales, TV shows, movies, and novels. Conventionally, the underdog wins; but Jerry loses, in an impossible fight against a vicious bully. According to Sylvia Iskander, 'When readers complain about Cormier's hopeless pessimism, they mean that the novel's close defies their expectations.'[4]

Iskander assumes that the expectations the novel thwarts relate to the conventions of fiction rather than to those of reality; we may *know* that underdogs don't always win in real life, but still find a novel in which one loses unpersuasive. It's interesting, therefore, that Cormier himself sees his defiance of fictional norms as exactly what makes his novels a more accurate representation of reality: 'As long as what I write is true and believable, why should I have to create happy endings? My books are an antidote to the TV view of life, where even in a suspenseful show you know before the last commercial that Starsky and Hutch will get their man. That's phony realism. Life just isn't like that.'[5]

Or is it? According to the novelist, *The Chocolate War* was based on a real situation. But in reality, Cormier wrote a letter supporting his son's decision not to take part in the school's chocolate sale: 'So, what happened is, he gave the letter to the headmaster, who read it and said, "Fine, Peter," and nothing happened.'[6]

Nothing happened: no isolated underdog like Jerry Renault, no villain like Archie Costello or Brother Leon, no corrupt secret society like the Vigils – and no unhappy ending. That Cormier imagined all this suggests just how much the book deviates not just from conventional stereotypes but also, despite Cormier's claims otherwise, from an accurate representation of reality. In fact, the essence of Cormier's genius in *The Chocolate War* is his masterful evocation of a nightmarishly intense atmosphere, a powerful and powerfully upsetting vision of hopelessness.

A first-time reader with knowledge only of the title of the book and its reference to war might well assume that the opening paragraphs do actually describe a battle:

> They murdered him.
> As he turned to take the ball, a dam burst against the side of his head and a hand grenade shattered his stomach.[7]

Only later does it become clear that the ball is a football, not gunshot, and that the grenade and the dam are metaphoric. The description of a perfectly ordinary football practice that follows contains comparisons to murder, mutiny, burning, gangsters, dams bursting and hand grenades exploding. Later in the book, paint peels 'like leprosy' (p. 13), leaves 'fluttered to the ground like doomed and crippled birds' (p. 114), and telephone dial tones explode or are 'like a fart in his ear' (p. 181). Cormier reserves the most loathsome similes for parts and products of the human body. Fingers are 'like the legs of pale spiders with a victim in their clutch' (p. 105). Eyes are like 'boiled onions' (p. 104) or 'like specimens in laboratory test tubes' (p. 82). Sweat is 'like small moist bugs' (p. 7), and the sound of vomiting is 'like a toilet being flushed' (p. 172). These continual ugly or violent comparisons charge fairly mundane events with demonic force.

Cormier also carefully selects the events that we view through the filter of these obsessively ugly comparisons. We hear almost nothing about the characters' families or life at home. We don't know what sort of parents produced a fiend like Archie or a bully like Emile Janza. The only parent who appears significantly in the book is Jerry's father, a defeated widower who pays little attention to his son. Cormier explains his omissions by sayings, 'People can't say Archie did this because he was a deprived child or he was a victim of child abuse. I wanted him judged solely on his actions.'[8] But he creates the impression that parents in general have little interest in their children, that most or even all children must face a hard world on their own.

What Cormier shows us is as carefully selected as what he leaves out. An omniscient third-person narrator tells the story, but always from the perspective of different characters; and there are frequent switches from one character's thoughts to another's, from how Jerry experiences his first football practice to how Obie thinks about it as he watches it from the stands. It seems logical to assume that during the course of events the book describes, many of characters whose thoughts appear in it would have had happy moments, or at least relaxing ones. But Cormier almost never allows us to experience such moments; as the focus of our attention switches from mind to mind, we track a carefully selected course of brutal or cowardly thoughts and actions, almost all obsessively concerned with the chocolate sale, and violent or despairing responses to them.

At one point or another in the novel, furthermore, we experience the perspectives of thirteen different people. The result of this constant switching between many different minds, only to discover that all the minds are thinking about the same subject and caught up in equally strong emotions about it, is the main source of book's intensity and of the distinctive claustrophobia of its atmosphere. It makes the events of the chocolate sale seem like the unswerving focus of everyone's attention.

It also creates a deep irony. We know what the characters do not know – that in the imprisoning isolation of each of their individual minds and deeply conscious of their isolation, they are all not only thinking about the same things but also having thoughts about it that are similar to each other.

Cormier magnifies this overall irony with detailed parallels and contrasts between the characters. In the first chapter, Jerry worries about getting on the good side of a powerful person, the coach; in the second, Obie worries about keeping the powerful Archie happy. In chapter five, Archie gives a 'performance' for the Vigils, 'toying with kids, leading them on, humiliating them' (p. 31), and in the next chapter, Brother Leon does exactly the same thing with the students in his class: 'Ten minutes left – time enough for Leon to perform, to play one of his games' (p. 39). Leon plays the game of singling out a bright student and accusing him of cheating; immediately after that, we discover how Emile Janza 'found that people had a fear of being embarrassed or humiliated, of being singled out for special attention' (p. 48). Like Leon, Emile 'found that the world was full of willing victims' (p. 47); but before the chapter is over, this bully is himself humiliated by Archie.

Later in the novel, Jerry and Goober discuss evil as they run through the streets (p. 149); in the next chapter as Leon and Archie discuss the chocolate problem, 'Leon's breath filled the gaps between the words as if he'd been running long distance' (pp. 153–4) and a few pages later, Cochran says 'I think Leon's on the run' (p. 155). As in this last example, Cormier often cross-cuts specific images and phrases as well as situations. On one page, Archie perceives that Leon 'was someone riddled with cracks and crevices . . . vulnerable, running scared, open to invasion' (pp. 22–3); a little later, the tables are turned as Leon himself watches his class, 'probing for weaknesses in the students and then exploiting those weaknesses' (p. 25). Leon singles out Bailey, 'looking at him as if he were a specimen under a microscope, as if the specimen contained the germ of some deadly disease' (p. 40); again the tables turn as Goober perceives that Leon himself has 'moist eyes like specimens in laboratory test tubes' (p. 82). Similarly, Jerry's eyes 'burned with fire, fuelled by lack of sleep' (p. 118) soon after he observes that Leon's eyes offer 'a glimpse into the hell that was burning inside the teacher' (p. 116).

In all these instances, the use of similar language for apparently different people and situations forces us to make connections between them, to see them part of the same obsessively claustrophobic atmosphere. In the most blatant example of his insistence on connecting everything, Cormier and various of his character use the word 'beautiful' to describe the photograph of a girl (p. 17), Emile Janza's beastly behaviour (p. 48), Goober's running (p. 51), the sight of a teacher getting upset (p. 65), a football pass (p. 75), America (p. 98), the sight of Emile masturbating (p. 99), the idea of not selling chocolates (p. 135), a girl (p. 149), the success of the chocolate sale (p. 187), Jerry's gullibility to Archie's final scheme (p. 169), Jerry's punch at Emile (p. 222), and Archie's final triumph (p. 150). With each further use, the word becomes more ambiguous – we can no longer be sure what it means, but we know it certainly isn't what we thought it meant before we read the book.

The intense atmosphere all this creates is hardly a balanced representation of reality. Some readers have suggested that *The Chocolate War* actually forces readers to *reject* its apparently negative conclusion. Sylvia Iskander believes that because of his divergence from fictional norms, 'Cormier makes his readers think long after they have closed his novels. . . . The climactic structure of his novels with their shocking, unhappy, but quite realistic endings reinforces not the temporary defeats or a bleak pessimism, but rather a longing for justice.'[9] Less convinced of Cormier's realism, Millicent Lenz nevertheless insists that 'the reader can react only with revulsion for such evil, and so desolate a vision, [and so] calls up a counter-vision of a possible better world – a world that lies within human will and choice to realize.'[10]

But in insisting that the proper response to *The Chocolate War* is to move beyond its distorted vision of reality, these commentators neglect that fact that many readers seem to want to respond to it by saying something like, 'Yes, that's just the way things are.' I suspect Cormier intends us to respond in just this way – although not necessarily because he intended the novel to be an *accurate* representation of the way things are.

To accept the novel's vision is to share Archie's belief that 'life is shit' (p. 16). In psychological terms, having that belief and taking comfort in it can be identified as paranoia. I believe that the horrific world of *The Chocolate War* represents a distorted, paranoid vision of the ways things are.

Paranoiacs assume, incorrectly, that they are the constant subject of the attention and hostility of others more powerful than themselves. In the real world, the fact that Cormier's son didn't want to sell chocolates was a matter of no interest; but in the delusional world of the novel, the refusal of one insignificant freshman becomes the major and only business of the school, the obsessive concern of everyone in authority. In other words, what is merely delusional in a paranoic is literally true for Jerry: everyone *is* out to get him.

According to Freud, a paranoic 'corrects some aspect of the world which is unbearable to him by the construction of a wish and introduces this delusion into reality.'[11] On first consideration, Jerry's horrific world hardly seems more bearable than the boring but relatively safe one inhabited by Cormier's son and by most teenagers; but its advantage is that in it Jerry *does* in fact matter enough to deserve attack – that despite his apparent insignificance and lack of power, he is important enough to demand the attention of those with power.

In more conventional wish-fulfilment fantasies, of course, the deserving underdog and the values he stands for would triumph: that is certainly what happens in earlier school stories like Kipling's *Stalky and Co.* to supposed underdogs like the disobedient but always victorious Stalky. But while Jerry may seem to be defeated, the viciousness of the attack on him merely proves what the hostility paranoiacs feel being directed toward themselves always proves – that he is important enough, enough of a threat to those in power for it to become necessary for them to crush him. It also confirms Jerry's own inherent blamelessness: it's clearly the corrupt viciousness of those in power that keeps Jerry a powerless victim, and therefore not his own guilt or inadequacy. For these reasons, the paranoid vision, in its very hopelessness, is a source of intense pleasure for readers.

The paranoid satisfactions of the plot are intensified by the novel's unusual manipulations of point of view. Because we follow the action as it passes through different minds, we continually find out that each of those minds is centrally concerned with how events will affect itself. We constantly experience different people seeing themselves as the centre of attention, each one imagining himself to be the one person who is the target of everyone else's hostility. Every one of the characters seems paranoid.

According to Freud, furthermore, paranoiacs often 'complain that all their thoughts are known and their actions watched and supervised.'[12] The characters of *The Chocolate War* obsessively think about watching and being watched throughout the book – watch each other for signs of hostility, and often feel they are being watched and their secrets being found out. Jerry observes Leon's eyes, 'eyes that reflected everything that went on in the class, reacting to everything. ... After Jerry had learned that the secret of Brother Leon lurked in his eyes, he became watchful, seeing the way the eyes betrayed the teacher at every turn' (p. 116). Similarly, Obie, observes 'something flash in Archie's eyes, like looking at a blank window and observing a ghost peeking out' (p. 140).

Each of the characters has a version of that ghost, a secret life at odds with the appearance he presents to the world. Tubs Casper thinks lustful thoughts about his girlfriend as he presents 'his most innocent and sweetest smile' to chocolate buyers (p. 91), and we hear that 'Archie was careful to keep his poker face, intent on not betraying an emotion. But he was shaken inside' (p. 170).

This sense of a difference between what the characters feel and what they show is the source of their paranoia. Knowing his own dark secrets, each of them suspects the others have the power to see them also – that everyone else is always watching, getting past the facade, ferreting out hidden inadequacies. As a result, the characters treasure dark, hidden places where they can't be seen. Jerry thinks of his bed as 'dark and safe and quiet' (p. 204), and Jerry's friend Goober of his bed as 'a private world, a small, safe place without people' (p. 237). To be safe is to be beyond observation.

At one point, Jerry hungrily observes a photograph of a girl in a magazine, then guiltily glances around 'to see if he'd been observed.' (p. 17) Later, Howie Andersen speaks of 'watching girls and devouring them with your eyes – rape by eyeball' (p. 134); in looking at the photograph and feeling guilty, Jerry is a visual rapist worried about being raped. A few paragraphs later, he discovers he *has* been observed – not observing the girl, but observing the hippies in the park. One of them accuses him of staring at them, and he must acknowledge to himself that he has been, that his guilty secret of observing others has been found out.

And this is the essence of the novel's cleverness, and the main source of its satisfaction it offers readers: here as throughout the novel apparently paranoid delusions are almost always confirmed. In *The Chocolate War* it's not a paranoid delusion that others are always watching you and finding out your guilty secrets: it's merely the truth.

Archie's genius for evil (and for that matter, Leon's) is simply to watch others carefully enough to find their weaknesses – then threaten to reveal them. Archie's status as a dangerous observer is established a few pages after Howie Anderson discusses 'rape by eyeball,' as Archie thinks of a girls' school where 'you could let your eyes devour some luscious sights' (p. 137). It's not surprising that he keeps Emile Janza in his power through the threat of a non-existent photograph of Emile masturbating behind the door of a washroom cubicle, a photograph that Emile worries might be observed by others just as Jerry observes the photograph of the girl: he fears rape by eyeball. Nor is it surprising that Emile enrages Jerry by accusing him of living 'in the closet' (p. 200), 'hiding that deep dark secret' (p. 201); Emile knows through personal experience that everyone likes 'in the closet' – hides dark secrets behind their facades.

Patricia Campbell describes the protagonist of Cormier's later novel *Fade* as 'a young boy on the verge of exploring adult sexuality, but with a penchant for voyeurism because he is by nature a shy observer. Quite early in the novel we see him setting a pattern of gratification from contemplating what is forbidden . . . . Because he is by nature a sexual spy it is no accident that the fade leads him to "dark and nasty secrets it was better not to know about."'[13] Many of the characters in *The Chocolate War* are also young boys on the verge of adult sexuality, also observers – and also discovering nasty secrets they think it better not to know about. But more significantly, *The Chocolate War*'s insistence on allowing us as readers to observe what goes on inside its characters' minds forces us also to become like Paul. Like him, we are shy voyeurs, invisible observers observing dark secrets.

If we find it uncomfortable to do that, even while enjoying the pleasures of the paranoid visions we are allowed to share, we are doing nothing more than responding to an ambiguity in the novel that seems to be deliberate. For as well as confirming the pleasures of paranoia, *The Chocolate War* seriously (and just as pleasurably) calls them into question.

One way it does so is by asking a question that relates significantly to paranoia: who is a victim? According to Archie, 'The world was made up of two kinds of people – those who were victims and those who were victimisers. There was no doubt about Janza's category. No doubt about himself either' (pp. 100–1). Given what we know of their behaviour, we have to assume that Archie sees both himself and Janza as victimisers. But we've just seen Archie victimising Janza over the matter of the photograph. And if Janza is a victim, then what of Archie himself? And what of Brother Leon?

It may not be merely ironic that David Caroni concludes 'that Brother Leon had been the victim' (p. 107), with Jerry his victimiser. Leon and Archie's characters are such that they could respond to Jerry's actions only by indulging in ever more loathsome acts of malevolence. In effect then, Jerry has unintentionally done for Archie and Leon what Emile always intentionally does to his victims: create circumstances in which they will reveal their secret vices and moral weaknesses. In this sense, Archie and Leon have been Jerry's victims.

We might understand that in Christian terms: Cormier is a practis-
ing Catholic. Thinking about Archie's victory over Jerry, Obie concludes it 'proves that the meek don't inherit the earth' (p. 224). But as
we've seen, in fact they do: like the apparently defeated Christ dying
on the cross, the meek Jerry wins by losing – becomes a hero for
readers by revealing the hopeless corruption of the world. And also
like Christ, Jerry is not apparently meek. His unyielding refusal to
do what he does not want to do implies strength rather than weakness,
and we must conclude that it's the people who meekly go along with
the corruptions of those with power who are actually the meek ones.
If we think of the novel in this way, we can conclude two things: the
truly meek do inherit the earth, to the extent that the meek conformists
aren't the ones victimised by Archie and his like; but since the only
apparently meek Jerry is so ruthlessly unyielding and since he really
does win, Obie was right in a way he didn't intend: the meekly
conventional don't inherit the earth after all.

And yet – All this assumes that the paranoic vision is correct, that
Jerry's apparent meekness is actually strength. The novel also offers
evidence to undercut the paradox and suggest that it isn't. We see
Jerry constantly trying to hide, to fade, to be somewhere other than
where ugly things are happening. According to Campbell, 'Jerry is
inherently passive. His natural instincts are to do nothing. That is
why the poster that challenges him to disturb the universe is so
fascinating to him. The refusal to sell the chocolates only *seemed* like
a heroic action because of the circumstances that led up to it. Actually, once the refusal is set in motion, Jerry's natural inertia keeps it
in place.' (p. 70). In fact, Jerry's heroic action, his way of disturbing
the universe, is a negative decision not to act rather than a positive
decision to do something. Perhaps his meekness isn't heroic after all.

Furthermore, we're told that Janza 'had discovered a truth early in
life. . . . Nobody wanted trouble, nobody wanted to make trouble,
nobody wanted a showdown. The knowledge was a revelation. It
opened doors. You could take a kid's lunch or even his lunch money
and nothing usually happened because most kids wanted peace at
any price' (pp. 47–8). Jerry's desire to be passive clearly identifies
him with what Janza thinks of as 'willing victims' (p. 47). In a very
real sense, he invites the trouble that lead to his defeat, by trying to
avoid trouble.

Cormier says, 'I think the monstrous is so often disguised as
innocence.'[14] While he's talking about a character in *After the First
Death*, this comment might well refer to Jerry also. Archie quite

rightly says, 'Everybody has to do things in this world they don't want to' (p. 164); without compromise there's only anarchy. But Jerry won't accept that: he does something anti-social, an essentially meaningless act of defiance, for no clear reason other than that it *is* anti-social, the opposite of what the world wants and expects him to do. We might argue that the book gives evidence that this particular society is corrupt enough to need to be defied; but we shouldn't forget that it's Jerry's act of defiance which elicits the behaviour that seems so corrupt. While there's no doubt that Archie and Leon are flawed beings, there's no evidence that their malevolence would have become so intense had not Jerry unwittingly created the situation that threatened their status.

In this sense, then, Jerry's innocence *is* monstrous, a tempting invitation to evildoers. We might even say that Jerry has victimised himself. Certainly he victimises himself in falling for Archie's scheme of fighting Emile; using physical force to get even with his oppressors merely confirms his fellowship with people like Emile.

Cormier insists we realise that. As Jerry punches Emile, he tells us that 'a new sickness invaded Jerry, the sickness of knowing what he had become, another animal, another beast, another violent person in a violent world, inflicting damage, not disturbing the universe but damaging it'(p. 242). The victim turns into another victimiser.

An earlier and even more ironic confrontation between victims and victimisers similarly insists on the degree to which the innocent might be guilty. After Father Leon mercilessly victimises one of his students, he confronts the others with their own inadequacy in not coming to his defence: 'those of you who didn't enjoy yourselves allowed it to happen, allowed me to proceed. You turned this classroom into Nazi Germany for a few moments' (pp. 44–5). The irony, of course, is that Leon is both right and wrong – it was he himself who turned the class into Nazi Germany, victimised the students by creating a situation which would allow him to say truthfully that they were the victimisers.

The richest irony of this situation is that one of the obvious villains of the piece enunciates one of its important themes – that those who go along with villains allow villainy to happen. Brother Leon enunciates another important theme when he tries to get Caroni to sympathise with him by telling him, 'teachers are human too. Human like other people' (p. 104). Instead of sympathising, Caroni understands Leon's less than perfect behaviour toward him to mean that teachers are not as superior as he had hoped, but disappointingly

32   *Perry Nodelman*

'like everyone else' (p. 107). We are all capable of evil, and we must all live with what Caroni learns here: 'that there were no heroes, really, and that you couldn't trust anybody, not even yourself' (p. 87).

But Caroni concludes that therefore 'life was rotten' (p. 107), that the humanity of teachers means they are 'as corrupt as the villains you read about in books or saw in movies and television' (p. 107). For Caroni – and as we've seen, for some readers of the novel – the idea that all human beings are capable of evil is cause for despair or reason to indulge wholeheartedly in paranoid fantasy. In fact, *The Chocolate War* acknowledges the ever-present dangers of human fallibility without either being defeated by it or being content with the paranoia. As his insights into the dangers of Jerry's innocence suggest, Cormier actually seems to suggest that knowledge of that danger is exactly what best protects people from it.

For a long time, it seems, Cormier imagined his story to be complete. But in 1985, ten years after the publication of *The Chocolate War*, a sequel appeared. It often happens that the addition of a new item to a series changes the meaning of earlier items in the sequence, by making us think of them as causes for events we didn't at first have knowledge of. The mere existence of *Beyond the Chocolate War* implies that what seemed satisfyingly over was merely the incomplete prelude of further events that eventually lead to the *real* ending – that whatever we thought was the the meaning of the events of *The Chocolate War*, particularly those aspects of meaning we based on the way the book concluded, was inaccurate; or more exactly, that Cormier changed his mind about their meaning enough to wish to change it.

In many ways, *Beyond the Chocolate War* does subvert the meanings of *The Chocolate War*. Jerry fights Emile Janza again and emerges, he believes, the winner: the underdog finally triumphs. Archie and Leon, who remained unscathed during *The Chocolate War*, both receive punishment; both are threatened with death, and while both survive they also receive the punishment of being made to appear foolish, one as the designated Fool on Fair Day and the other as the target of a ripe tomato.

Indeed, the new events of *Beyond the Chocolate War* might well be seen as an attempt to normalise the situation – to provide something more like the happy ending readers expect of children's fiction. In many ways, *Beyond the Chocolate War* is more conventional than its predecessor – its language less ornate, its focus and mood less broodingly intense. There are fewer similes and metaphors. Our attention focuses on a smaller number of characters seen for longer periods of time, and a widening of scope dissipates the suffocating claustrophobia of *The Chocolate War*, as we learn that the boys have more connections outside the school than we were allowed to know about before. There are scenes involving Goober and his father, the new character Ray Bannister and his father and mother, David Caroni and his father, mother and brother. We find out that both Obie and Archie have girlfriends, and that the girls occupy surprisingly many of their thoughts. Many scenes take place in homes and on the street, away from the claustrophobic atmosphere of Trinity itself.

Furthermore, the novel is decidedly less paranoid. Instead of all the characters worrying constantly and ineffectively about the hostility of others towards them, we follow the thoughts of those bent on revenge – people thinking about actively responding to belligerence rather than merely expecting it and waiting for it to happen. During the course of the novel, Carter seeks revenge against Archie, Obie against Archie and Bunting, David Caroni against Brother Leon, Archie against Leon, Obie and Carter, Jerry against Emile.

As a result, the characters worry as frequently in the sequel as they did in the original about hiding their true thoughts from others; but whereas in *The Chocolate War* they wished to hide private guilt or inadequacy, here they often wish to hide their ill intentions towards others; as Obie fools Ray Bannister, he feels that his friendly smile is 'plastered' on, 'like a label . . . on a stick of dynamite,'[15] and Carter and Obie both worry that Archie can see their guilt in turning against him.

But these apparent reversals actually reinforce the subtly ambiguous implication of the first novel. In fact, closer consideration reveals that *Beyond the Chocolate War* merely makes the meaning and significance of *The Chocolate War* more obvious.

We've already seen how Jerry Renault's apparent loss in *The Chocolate War* is a victory; in *Beyond the Chocolate War*, his victory is clearly proclaimed, as he refuses to lash back at Emile and then says, 'Janza was beating me up. But he wasn't winning. I mean, you can get beat up and not lose. You can look like a loser but don't have to be one' (p. 223).

At the end of *The Chocolate War*, Jerry has already realised that fighting back against a fighter is yourself becoming what you were fighting. In *Beyond the Chocolate War*, character after character makes similar realisations in a much more obvious way. In fighting Archie,

Carter concludes 'He had become one of the things he'd always hated' (p. 101); Obie too realises 'what had happened to him. What Archie had done to him. He had driven him to the point of murder' (p. 261). While David Caroni never realises it, he too clearly becomes what he hates in his attack on Leon; and his action of seeking revenge against Brother Leon and then destroying himself is a luridly intensified variation on Jerry's metaphorically suicidal decision in *The Chocolate War* to seek revenge against the brutal Janza, which results in Janza's 'murdering' him. (Furthermore, David's death ties the two novels together simply by happening – it is as inevitable and as unexpected a defeat of an underdog as was Jerry's loss in *The Chocolate War*.)

Beyond the Chocolate War most clearly insists that revenge against evil is merely going in to the evil by cleverly establishing situations in which we as readers must make the same realisation that Jerry and Carter and Obie do. Knowing the depths of Leon and Archie's corruption, and having some familiarity with the literary convention that evildoers deserve every punishment an author can think of giving them, we come to expect and even hope that David Caroni will kill Leon and Obie murder Archie. Then, as Obie perceives the ugly significance of his own wish to murder Archie and David's death emerges as an inevitable consequence of his attempt to punish Leon, we must consider the significance of our hope that they succeed in their vicious acts of revenge – the significance of what our own response to Leon's and Archie's evil has made *us* become.

Furthermore, Cormier makes clear here what Jerry only vaguely implies at the end of *The Chocolate War* – that people like Archie and Leon are not the ones who cause evil in the world. In *The Chocolate War*, as Jerry realises his own complicity in evil and thinks about 'what he had become,' he tells himself 'He had allowed Archie to do this to him' (p. 242). In *Beyond the Chocolate War*, when Obie asks, 'What have I become?' (p. 209) and Obie wonders 'what had happened to him' (p. 261), both merely blame Archie for it. Archie himself points out the more subtle truth that Jerry realised in the earlier novel; he tells Obie, 'You could have said *no* anytime, anytime at all. But you didn't. . . . Free choice, Obie, and you did the choosing' (p. 264).

Furthermore, despite Cormier's clever trickery in setting up these situations, we as readers didn't *have* to wish Leon and Archie dead, or even that Archie might suffer more in his role as the Fool; we *chose* to gave in to that easy triumph. We too are guilty – that is, human, and therefore capable of evil, just as we were implicated in the paranoid act of watching in *The Chocolate War*.

Nor is it accidental that it's Archie who makes this clear. In *The Chocolate War* also it was a villain, Leon, who enunciated the idea that the apparently innocent were not so innocent. In a particularly ironic repetition at the end of *Beyond the Chocolate War*, Brother Leon tells the students of Trinity that they in their lack of involvement are as guilty of David Caroni's death as he himself is. Earlier, when he told his class that they in their silence were as guilty for his brutalising of Gregory Bailey as he himself was, he seemed right. Now in retrospect we have to wonder if he wasn't being as self-indulgent then as he is now; in both cases he quite happily forgives himself. Just as Leon's comments can be turned against himself, so too can Archie's. He too has chosen to be who and what he is, and may be dismissed and reviled for making the wrong choice.

Finally then, *Beyond the Chocolate War* makes clear what *The Chocolate War* already implied – that the propensity of boys in school to do cruel blackguard things is merely the potential in us all to do evil. Singly or together, the two novels not only reveal what cruelty always has been and always will be done in schools, and wherever else human beings gather; they also provide readers with surprisingly subtle and highly entertaining insights into the meaning of that cruelty.

NOTES

1. Thomas Hughes, *Tom Brown's Schooldays*, (1856; Harmondsworth, Middlesex: Penguin Puffin, 1971), p. 64.
2. A *Junior Bookshelf* reviewer angrily complained that Cormier's story of the events surrounding Trinity School's fund-raising chocolate sale 'depicts a life without hope in which boys prey upon each other like prohibition gangsters, masturbate in the lavatory and drool over girlie magazines' (quoted in Patricia J. Campbell, *Presenting Robert Cormier* [New York: Dell Laurel Leaf, 1985, 1989], p. 53). In a review in *Booklist*, Betsy Hearne suggested that Cormier 'manipulates readers into believing how rotten things are by loading the dice while pretending to play fair' ('Whammo, You Lose' *Booklist*, July 1974, p. 1199). Norma Bagnall says, 'Only the ugly is presented through the novel's language, actions, and imagery; goodness and honour are never rewarded. Love and concern for other people is ignored, and hopelessness pervades the entire story.' She adds, 'We can teach hopelessness to our young if they are taught that no matter how hard they struggle they cannot win. This story teaches that hopelessness' ('Realism: How Realistic Is it? A Look at *The Chocolate War*,' *Top of the News* 36, Winter 1980, 214).

3.   Campbell, p. 58.
4.   Sylvia Patterson Iskander, 'Readers, Realism, and Robert Cormier,' *Children's Literature* 15 (1987), 12.
5.   Paul Janeczko, 'In their Own Words: An Interview with Robert Cormier,' *English Journal* 66 (September 1977), 11.
6.   Geraldine De Luca and Roni Natov, 'An Interview with Robert Cormier,' *The Lion and the Unicorn* 2,2 (Fall 1978), 109.
7.   De Luca, 122.
8.   Robert Cormier, *The Chocolate War* (New York: Pantheon, 1974), p. 3.
9.   Iskander, 18.
10. Millicent Lenz, 'A Romantic Ironist's Vision of Evil: Robert Cormier's *After the First Death,' Proceedings of the Eight Annual Conference of the Children's Literature Association* (Boston: Northeastern University, 1981), p. 52.
11. Sigmund Freud, *Civilisation and Its Discontents*, trans. James Strachey (New York: Norton, 1962), p. 28.
12. Sigmund Freud, *The Freud Reader*, ed. Peter Gay (New York: Norton, 1989), p. 559.
13. Campbell, p. 153.
14. De Luca, 132.
15. Robert Cormier, *Beyond the Chocolate War* (New York: Knopf, 1985), p. 29.

3
Home and Family: English and American Ideals in the Nineteenth Century

GILLIAN AVERY

'But we did not think those English children had so good a time as we did;' wrote Lucy Larcom of her Massachusetts childhood in the 1830s. 'They had to be so prim and methodical. 'It seemed to us that the little folks across the water never were allowed to romp and run wild; some of us may have held a vague idea that this freedom of ours was the natural inheritance of republican children only.'[1] A child in an early American travelogue,[2] on a visit to England commented, in much the same way, that her English contemporaries seemed to be brought up with infinitely more rigours, but 'they cannot take care of themselves half so well as the juvenile Americans'. One also remembers the glimpse that Louisa Alcott gives us of well-born young 'Englishers' in chapter XII of *Little Women*. We pass over the way young Fred cheats at croquet; that surely was not typical, but the twenty-year-old Kate's 'stand-off-don't-touch-me air, which contrasted strongly with the free-and-easy demeanour of the other [Amercian] girls' is instantly recognisable. It was indeed the manner implicitly prescribed in books for British girlhood such as those of Charlotte Yonge, and, caricatured, can be seen in all its perfection in Trollope's Griselda Grantley (destined to be the Marchioness of Hartletop), the nonpareil of English female decorum. Hippolyte Taine, who visited England in the 1860s, had remarked upon how the adolescent daughters of the upper classes, though they might look well-grown, were still children, 'Not one of their ideas or gestures betray the woman'.[3]

Dinner at 'Mistress T – 's; her two nieces dined with us. Very simple, schoolgirlish dresses. The elder hardly raised her eyes

throughout the meal, or did so briefly and shyly. . . . Their silence is
due to nothing but shyness, a childish modesty, the simple wild
timidity of a startled doe. When you speak to them they blush.[4]

Expecting this sort of self-effacement in their daughters, English
parents found the easy assurance and self-command of the American young woman monstrous and against nature: 'I do not recollect
to have seen a bashful girl in the United States',[5] said an outraged
mid-Victorian visitor. In this connection the reader remembers the
teasing romps beloved of many American authors in the last century
– Rose Red in Susan Coolidge's *What Katy Did At School* (1873) is a
well-known example, a teenager with a ready, even impudent tongue
and with a penchant for inventive mischief. As shown here they are
appealing; on English soil they would seem dangerously bold.

Almost all European travellers commented on the assertive independence of the American child. From earliest settler days the
youngest had had their part to play in the household economy and
the feeling of equality had never been lost. Some foreigners
commended this quality; more thought it against nature. Isabella
Bird said that American juveniles were completely destitute of 'that
agreeable shyness which prevents English and Scotch children from
annoying strangers'.[6] Harriet Martineau on the other hand found it
enchanting, though she was one of the many who protested at the
way American parents ruined the digestion and health of their
children by allowing them far too much rich food. But in the main
she approved of the way they were brought up, and attributed their
good temper to the way they had been managed in childhood, 'with
an easy freedom and friendliness between parent and child'.[7] Most
young English readers appeared to feel a similar admiration for the
transatlantic manner, judging by the popularity in this country of
writers such as Louisa Alcott, Susan Coolidge, Margaret Sidney and
Kate Douglas Wiggin, and of magazines like *St Nicholas* and *Harper's
Young People*. The liberated atmosphere of the American family books
in the last century, and the robust and confident children, from Jacob
Abbott's Rollo to the little friends-of-all-the-world like Pollyanna,
and Rebecca of Sunnybrook Farm, fascinated young Britons, who
could find nothing comparable in their own books. Here, until the
advent of E. Nesbit's more independent families, characters moved
always under the watchful and anxious eyes of parents.

It is ironical that the English traveller of the last century had
denied that there were any childlike children in the United States.

(Conversely, they had assumed that the playfulness and innocent high spirits of their own were seen and admired by all visitors). 'Little America is, unhappily, only grown-up America seen through a telescope turned the wrong way,' said one visitor sadly,[8] mentioning the way in which boys devoured newspapers and talked politics, and how the little girls 'talked toilette' and gossiped and descanted on the merits of the latest French novel. Other visitors commented on how early commercial instincts manifested themselves, and how children began to trade and make money as soon as they understood anything. 'I never discovered that there were any American *children*. Diminutive men and women in process of growing up into big ones, I have met with, but the child, in the full sense attached to that word in English, a child with its rosy cheeks and bright, joyous laugh, its docile obedience and simplicity, its healthful play and its disciplined work, is a being almost unknown in America.'[9]

Part of the trouble was that these commentators tended to meet only city children, and to base their judgements largely on the precocious and untypical specimens they encountered in hotels – there was a period when a certain type of urban American family took up residence in hotels, presumably because it solved the problem of finding servants. But there was also a difference of what the Old World and the New World expected of its young. The English wanted them to be obedient, well-disciplined, deferential to adults, and above all childlike. There should be (within marked limits, of course) the spontaneity of Rousseau's child and the artless joy of Blake's. But all should be carefully trained on a frame of Christian duty, and be subject to instant obedience and submission to authority. Contrary to what Lucy Larcom supposed, the early and mid-Victorians expected their children to play. It was an innocent interlude in the serious course of life, in much the same way as recreation was mandatory under a convent regime. Their young, if the parents could afford it, were brought up secluded from the adult world; for girls this state was prolonged until they emerged from the schoolroom at eighteen, while for boys it could be said to last all through their university days. Upper class children were reared in conditions of considerable austerity; comfort was thought to be enervating to the character as well as to the physique, and this applied to their diet also. In Mrs Molesworth's *Mary* (1893) a mother visiting a confectioner's shop orders a glass of milk and a bun for her small daughter ('little Miss Bertram of the Priory'). But a stout lady coming in with her children says: 'Now, what will you have, my loveys? Puffs, cheesecakes, macaroons?' We are instantly aware that the family is a vulgar one and are prepared for their subsequent boorish behaviour. The early and mid-Victorian family stories reflect the rigours, moral and physical, then thought appropriate. Often strikingly well-written, with deft characterisation, they seem oppressive now in the lofty demands that they make on the child. Take Mrs Gatty's short story 'Rabbits' Tails' (*Aunt Judy's Tales*, 1859) for instance. In this lesson on the need for submission to God's will, supposedly addressed by an older sister to young siblings, two motherless small children, marooned in the nursery at the top of their grandmother's house, create a whole mythology round a collection of rabbits' tails, of which they become so obsessively fond that the grown-up world decides the fancy has gone too far and the tail must be swept away. The narrator is briskly dismissive of her listeners' anguish at the sadness of this story – 'What a waste of good emotions it was.' To her the real sorrow lies in the opportunity that was lost to improve the occasion, which could have been used for associating this insignificant loss with their other, far greater bereavement, and telling them 'that it would not please their dear mother at all for them to fret for her, and fancy they couldn't do without her, and be discontented because God had taken her away, and think it would have been much better for them if He had not done so . . . but that it would please her very much for them to pray to God to make them good.'

Writers such as Jean Ingelow, Annie Keary, Elizabeth Sewell and Charlotte Yonge undoubtedly thought they were showing childlike children, but the modern reader is struck by the degree of moral responsibility expected even of the youngest. They were entirely dependent upon adult decrees and no initiative was expected or allowed (one remembers how Miss Yonge could make a whole book, *P's and Q's, or the Question of Putting Upon*, 1872, turn upon whether a father would give his permission for his teenage daughters to attend early celebrations of Holy Communion), but they are the custodians of their consciences, and many stories dwell on the agony of mind suffered when they have committed some small wrong. In 'The Grandmother's Shoe' (*Stories Told to a Child*, 1860) Jean Ingelow describes the tormenting guilt that wracks Sophia after she has eaten half a windfall apricot. She has been forbidden to pick fruit, but does this rank as disobedience? She feels that the thunderstorm next day is the voice of God rebuking her. In *The Children's Tabernacle* (1871) by A.L.O.E. a family of children, convalescing from whooping cough, while away the time by making a model of the

Israelites' Tabernacle (carefully following the specifications in Exodus). When it is finished it will be shown to children from a ragged school as a Christmas treat. But Dora is carried away by enthusiasm and stitches the curtains on a Sunday, arguing that it is a work of charity and therefore permissible. At first, appalled by the way she has broken the fourth commandment, she considers unpicking the embroidery, but as she neglects to do this her life for the next few months is poisoned by the guilty secret, until she at last confesses it. Sometimes the guilt and remorse can last a lifetime, as in the short story within Annie Keary's *The Rival Kings, or Overbearing* (1857). An ungracious, surly brother finds he tries too late to apologise to his little sister, but she will not open her eyes – she is dead.

> Edward is now a grown-up man. He is a grave, quiet man. No one has ever known him go into a passion, or heard him say a hasty word; but if ever he sees brothers and sisters quarrelling, or sees one child taking an unfair advantage over another, there comes a stern, sad look on his face, and his voice trembles when he speaks to them.

However, says the author, it was fortunate for Edward 'that it was only a little, weak body that his bad temper killed, and not an immortal soul'. *The Rival Kings* is in fact a remarkable story of tensions between two families. It does not flinch from describing the passionate hatred of which children are capable and which in this case nearly results in the death of two of them. It is forceful and exciting, though one suspects that child readers, far from trying to correct their own tendencies to quarrel and take sides, would be led into violent partisanship by the very power of the characterisation. Nor is it comfortable reading; the author is severe on her characters. 'It was perhaps as well for all the children,' she ends, 'that the consequences of their faults lasted long enough to keep alive the remembrance of them after the first excitement had passed away.'

Later Victorians, often remembering the sternness of their own upbringing and the moral pressure put upon them, tried to make amends by peopling their books with irresponsible nursery scamps and pickles. But their mischievous escapades nearly always took place with a secure background of protective parents and nurses, and there were people to clear up the mess and mend the torn clothes; young Americans would still have found them amazingly helpless and childlike. There are a few exceptions, like the more robust children of Juliana Horatia Ewing, precursors of Nesbit, who though they have mid-Victorian consciences are capable of acting independently of adults, as, for instance, the two boys in *A Great Emergency* (1877) who run off on a canal barge because their own lives are so depressingly uneventful. (There is a moral here; while they are away a real emergency happens at home and the narrator feels lifelong remorse that he was not at hand to help.)

But even Mrs Ewing's excellent stories had only a limited readership; they failed to have the universal appeal that American books of the period often achieved. The trouble would seem to have been that the complex Victorian social stratification (particularly within the middle class), which was such a rich source of material for the adult novelist, had a deadening effect on children's books. Throughout much of the last century juvenile publishing was divided into two categories, books for Sunday schools and cottage homes, and books for what Charlotte Yonge termed the 'drawing-room' child. The subject matter, the ethic, and the style were totally different (Mrs Ewing's style, leisurely, discursive and given to abstraction, in particular could only be appreciated by those who had a good literary background), and it was not thought that either group could profit from reading about the other. The street waif stories of such writers as Hesba Stretton with their strong evangelical message (given to well-to-do children as Sunday reading) did to a certain extent break across the class barriers, and these – if one excludes Lewis Carroll – were probably the most popular British juvenile exports then. Many of them were well written and gave a stark and reasonably accurate picture of the life of the urban poor. But they allowed for no escape. To English writers, one's lot in life was God-ordained and it was profoundly presumptuous to expect to move out of it. The best that could happen to a poor boy was that he should be taught a trade and be enabled to earn an honest living. There was none of the heady optimism of the American rags-to-riches story, or the unlikely outcome of such books as Margaret Sidney's *Five Little Peppers and How They Grew* (1881) where a poor family is taken into a rich household and all live together in perfect harmony.

This mingling of the classes, even at a make-believe level, would have been unthinkable in an English book. Nor was it merely a question of the rich and the poor. Here the background, outlook and way of life were all so totally dissimilar that an author would not trouble to point them out. But even within the middle classes there were many elements that were apparently incompatible. The women who wrote for children appeared to be fighting a desperate rear-guard action against new money and mercantile values. Their instinct was that disinterested and honourable conduct, truth-telling, straightforwardness, were the birthright of the landed classes and those descended from them, and that devious behaviour and commercial instincts must be expected from those who were in contact with money. Both Charlotte Yonge (1823–1901) and Mrs Molesworth (1839–1921) were particularly concerned with demarcation of class territory. Miss Yonge, whose father owned a small estate in Hampshire, felt passionately that the Church of England and the English squirearchy were the guardians of religious truth and the right way of living, and that any contact with trade or the newly rich could only contaminate. Mrs Molesworth's father on the other hand, though he came from the right sort of family, resigned his army commission and became a Manchester business man, which no doubt accounts for his daughter's intense preoccupation with social status and self-conscious identification with the upper classes. She is, for instance, quick to stress that if the children eat their midday dinner with their parents, then it is of course the grownup's luncheon (lest any think she came from a household that had their main meal midday). Not all her stories are about wealthy nurseries, but she is always careful to explain that though her children may not be smartly dressed, they come from the right background. Little Miss Peggy, in the book of that name, found lost on a country road, is instantly identifiable as 'a little lady, though [she] looked miserable enough with her torn clothes, and scratched and tear-stained face.' Mrs Molesworth, writing in the last decades of the century, was far less severe on young children than her predecessors. They are comforting books, since she understood children's craving for security and affection, and only castigated them if they were discontented or fretful or unkind. But their readership was limited even at the time of publication, and has vanished now.

American writers for children on the other hand spent little time delineating the social background of their characters, and their characters, to an English eye, all displayed a marked degree of self-sufficiency. Few families, unless they lived in the South, had resident servants, and certainly not the sort of establishment that the English middle class took as the norm. The children, at any rate those in the country – which was where most writers chose to set their books – all had their duties to perform, and in the absence of nursemaids there could be no separate nursery life. Jacob Abbott (1803–79), a former schoolmaster who turned out 180 books (and 31 more of which he was joint-author or editor), was the first writer to make the American domestic scene familiar to English readers. He adapted the educational principles of Maria Edgeworth and her father, of letting the child learn practical skills and moral truths through experience and experiment, carrying it rather further so that in his stories there is remarkably little adult presence; it is usually not a parent who supervises but an older child. This youthful sage is sometimes a hired boy, and in one series 'a nice and tidy-looking coloured girl', but there is never any question of different social status; age and experience are what counts, and the younger children pay great attention to the advice and the instructions of the mentor. Abbott's aim was to produce capable, self-reliant children, who questioned, discovered and thought for themselves. They learn early how to manage money. The children in *Florence and John* (1860) get half a dollar weekly allowance, and if they propose an expedition they themselves have to pay part of the cost of hiring a carriage, and must undertake all the necessary arrangements, including the buying of the rail tickets and deciding upon a hotel. Moreover, they must agree to accept the consequences of their mistakes or else hand back the control to their mother. The pace of Abbott's chronicles is very leisurely, and there is little in the way of drama, but the domestic life is delightful; from him English children got their first glimpses of American pastimes that were to become increasingly familiar with Abbott's successors – blueberrying expeditions, sledging, making candy, maple sugaring.

Homely details were never so prominent in English books; indeed the great advantages that Americans had when it came to writing family stories was their passionate feeling for home and domesticity. From earliest times home had been a focus of emotion, representing in settler days a refuge from the harsh outside world, and latterly a temple presided over by the mother, the high priestess who alone could keep wanderers from being dragged down by the world's temptations. 'It is [women's] office to fulfill the "home mission" – to encourage virtue and piety in the household circle, and when sin and degradation enter, to bring their whole energies to the work of salvation.'[10] For Americans, the household community was a microcosm of the ideal republic they saw themselves to have created; all its members were independent and working towards the same purpose, for the good of the whole. A writer of 1785 imagined a European traveller encountering this perfection for the first time in a log house newly established in what had been wilderness six years before.

Each one in the family filled his own place, and contentment and satisfaction reigned through the whole. After family prayer, which was religiously attended, I retired to my lodging, with a disposition better suited to reflection than to sleep. I fancied myself to have fallen upon a discovery, after which the sages of antiquity had sought in vain. And that here in the wilderness, I had found in what the greatest happiness of life consisted. For here was religion without colour of superstition, – here was civil and religious liberty in perfection, – here was independence . . . here fullness was enjoyed in retirement – and the whole shut out from the disagreeable noise and bustle of the world.[11]

Some sixty years the log-house way of life was still an Amercian ideal. An 1844 reading primer showed a family living in perfect harmony and self-sufficiency:

Soon the table is ready. Bowls of fresh milk are upon it and bread that the mother has just baked, and eggs from their own poultry, and a cup of maple molasses. The father asks Heaven's blessing upon their food. Then, seated around, they partake it with cheerful hearts. . . .

They have brought from their home in New England, a few books which they highly prize. These the father reads to his wife at evening, while she knits or spins at his side; and from them she instructs their children, when he is at work in the fields, by day.

The one that they most value, is the Bible, the book of their Father in Heaven. They teach its blessed words to their little ones. They read it together, before they retire to rest, and then the father prays to God to protect and bless his family, and make them at last a family in heaven.[12]

We have here that mingling of piety with domestic comfort that was to feature so prominently in the American domestic novel. And we might also notice the emphasis on food, another characteristic, and one that was always to enchant young English readers, brought up austerely on a diet in which boiled mutton, potatoes, rice pudding and bread and milk played the most prominent part. Their American contemporaries were allowed to eat the same things as their parents, no matter how rich and unwholesome, and much of it seems to consist of food that appealed most to childish tastes, like pies, cakes, muffins, hot bread (spread thick with butter, a commodity not much in evidence in the English nursery, being thought unwholesome) and maple syrup.[13] English readers were wont to remember with a particular anguish the sacrifice of the Christmas breakfast that the March girls were called upon to make in an early chapter of *Little Women* – the muffins and cream and buckwheat cakes that were packed up and taken to a poor immigrant family. Even in moments of stress the food was not forgotten. It is notable, for instance, that in a crisis in Susan Warner's *The Wide, Wide World* (1850), the heroine has time to savour 'pot-pie' and to meditate over its excellence. (She has galloped over to bring a doctor to a neighbour who has broken his leg, but the doctor's housekeeper insists that she should refresh herself before she goes back.)

> The pieces of crust were white and light like new bread; the very tit-bits of meat she culled out for Ellen, and the soup gravy poured over all would have met even [her aunt's] wishes, from its just degree of richness and exact seasoning. Smoking hot, it was placed before Ellen on a little stand by her easy chair, with some nice bread and butter; and presently Miss Janet poured her out a cup of tea.

Ellen Montgomery is the type of heroine that no English writer of that period would have allowed herself. She is a titillating combination of the demure and the forward, a fascinating orphan who dissolves into tears upon the slightest provocation – tears that have a melting effect on every male who witnesses them, and many kisses and caresses are chastely exchanged. To ensure that they are chaste, Miss Warner by a device that some might call jesuitical, deems that Ellen's male guardian angel should style himself her 'brother', though it is implied at the close that when she is of nubile age he will come and claim her as his bride. Her novels in fact, though they were given away as Sunday school prizes, have a strong erotic element and a degree of self-indulgence that was not to be found in English books. But this undoubtedly made them very attractive to their girl readers, who also relished a transatlantic style of heroine, unburdened by parents, merely with an aunt to whom she is morally superior.

There were to be many in her mould. The pattern of the orphan facing a harsh world alone had no doubt come from England in the first instance, from Richardson and Charlotte Brontë and the very popular anonymous *Fatherless Fanny, or the little mendicant* (1811). But it was not one used much in English books for the young, unless they were about waifs and strays. We can trace the chain of American girl orphans from Catharine Maria Sedgewick's Jane Elton in *A New England Tale* (1822) and Ellen Bruce in *Redwood* (1824) by the same author. Meek, much-enduring, yet of far finer material than those about them, they have a spirit that eventually wins over the granite-hearted aunts that are also a feature of these tales. As the years went by the fashion changed. Meekness and tears were less favoured, and there was more emphasis on spirit and originality. Kate Douglas Wiggin's Rebecca (1903), L. M. Montgomery's Anne of Green Gables (1908) and Eleanor H. Porter's Pollyanna (1913), all recognisably sisters, are highly articulate and persuasive, and adored by those perceptive enough to recognise their distinctive qualities. There is also Jerusha in Jean Webster's *Daddy Long-Legs* (1912). Despite the fact that she has been brought up in an orphanage until she is 17, she has the brio of all American heroines of her type, and the literary flair which by this period was becoming an added attraction. The story ends in romance – another feature which distinguished books of this kind from their English contemporaries.

But all American heroines required household skills, and if they did not possess them in the beginning, had to acquire them; sometimes a painful process. It was stressed over and over again that American life was chancy, that the family with immense wealth one day might be penniless the next, and that all girls must be ready to turn their hand to the daily chores, and in particular should learn to cook. (In real life this had happened to Susan Warner, whose father lost all his money in a business crash. She and her sister were to spend the rest of their lives struggling to keep the family going on their meagre literary earnings). There was too a strong sense of the superiority of country values, and many plots turned on how a reverse of fortune and the resultant departure from the city brought about benefit for all. Or neurotic, pampered city children become robust and independent once they spend a few months on a farm. Very often the redemption is achieved with the help of food. Harriet Beecher Stowe's Pussy (blessed, like Pollyanna, from earliest infancy with the gift of always seeing the bright side of things) effects the transformation of the peevish, wilting daughter to a rich New York business man. We know from the first breakfast she brings Emily how matters will turn out.

First there was a large saucer of strawberries, delightfully arranged on green vine-leaves; then there was a small glass pitcher
full of the thickest and richest cream, that was just the colour of a
saffrano rose-leaf. . . . Then there was the most charming little cake
of golden butter you ever saw, shaped with a flower on it and
arranged upon two large strawberry-leaves, that actually had a
little round pearl of dew on each of their points. . . . Then there
were some white, tender little biscuits, and some nice round muffins
of a bright yellow colour, made of corn meal, by a very choice
receipt on which Pussy prided herself.[14]

This domestic element was virtually unknown in the English book of
the period and for a long time afterwards. Even in E. Nesbit's books
the children accept the meals placed before them without any thought
of how they are prepared. However pinched the circumstances seem
to be – as in *The Railway Children* – there is always someone to stew
the mutton. In the novels of the Charlotte Yonge and her kind it is a
drawing-room culture; the girl is shown in the schoolroom, by her
mother's safe (the Victorian mother was often in delicate health and
exacted endless small duties from her daughters); occasionally
teaching in the parish school. To some extent this tradition has
persisted; the background of such twentieth-century family stories
as Enid Blyton's and Noel Streatfeild's is above rather than below
stairs. Streatfeild families are not rich, but there are loyal retainers
who staff the kitchen. But it is the kitchen dimension that gives such
a pleasurable sense of warmth and comfort to the American family
books. The kitchen, not the drawing room, is the heart of the home.
Kenneth Grahame knew that he was about when the Rat and the
Mole stumble upon Badger's home and are brought in from the
horrors of the Wild Wood to 'all the glow and warmth of a large fire-
lit kitchen'. Few of his compatriots have been able to achieve the
same effect with human characters, and the most appealing English
kitchens are peopled, not by human families but by hobbits or moles;
by Mrs Tiggy-Winkle and Mrs Tabitha Twitchit and their kind. It
might even be significant that the most memorable of all, the Duch-
ess's kitchen in *Alice*, is a symbol of anarchy.

NOTES

1. Lucy Larcom: *A New England Girlhood* (Boston, 1889), p. 104.
2. Eliza Leslie: *The Young Americans, or Sketches of a Sea Voyage* (Boston, 1829).
3. Hippolyte Taine: *Notes on England* [1872]. Trs. Edward Hyams (London, 1957), p. 71.
4. Ibid., p. 69.
5. Thomas Grattan: *Civilised America* (London, 1859), vol. II, p. 57.
6. [Isabella Bishop]: *The Englishwoman in America* (London, 1856), p. 241.
7. Harriet Martineau: *Society in America* (London, 1837), vol. III, p. 173.
8. Lady Emmeline Stuart Wortley: *Travels in the United States* (London, 1851), vol. I, p. 269.
9. Thérèse Yelverton: *Teresina in America* (London, 1875), p. 263.
10. [Mrs Sarah Carter Edgarton Mayo]: *Ellen Clifford, or The Genius of Reform* (Boston, 1838).
11. [Thomas Brockway]: *The European Traveller in America* (Hartford, 1785).
12. Lydia Sigourney: *The Pictorial Reader* (New York, 1844).
13. Sometimes, however, enlightened authority decreed a plainer diet; Louisa Alcott's Dr Alec in *Eight Cousins* throws away his niece's strong coffee and makes her drink milk, and substitutes porridge and brown bread for her breakfast hot rolls.
14. Harriet Beecher Stowe: 'Little Pussy Willow' in *Stories and Sketches for the Young* (Boston, 1897).

4
'The Most Beautiful Things in All the World'? Families in *Little Women*

ELIZABETH LENNOX KEYSER

'I do think that families are the most beautiful things in all the world!' exults Jo March at the end of Louisa May Alcott's *Little Women* (1868–9).[1] Many readers have interpreted the novel as an argument, more or less convincing, for Jo's assertion. And if their own families have been less than beautiful, they may have responded wistfully as did Jean Muir, the heroine of Alcott's sensation story *Behind a Mask* (1866), on assuming her position as governess: 'Something in the atmosphere of this happy home has made me wish I was anything but what I am.'[2] Jo, however, utters her exclamation while 'in an unusually uplifted frame of mind' (p. 595), and Jean goes on in her next breath to declare 'Bah! how I hate sentiment!' (p. 99) Alcott's conflicted, problematical relationship with her own family, which she idealised in *Little Women* but satirised in *Transcendental Wild Oats* (1873), as well as her choice to remain single, suggest that she viewed the Victorian family realistically, if not sceptically. Further, Jean's uncharacteristic wish points to the danger of sentimentalising home and family, especially for women: it serves to make them dissatisfied with what they are and severely limits what they can become.

Having just read proofs for *Little Women*, Alcott wrote in her journal, 'we really lived most of it; and if it succeeds that will be the reason of it.'[3] The story of Alcott's own family is well known, though only recently have biographers begun to dwell on its darker side.[4] Her father, Transcendentalist educator and philosopher Bronson Alcott, engaged Louisa and her three sisters in Socratic dialogues and disciplined them by temporarily withdrawing his affection and approval. The docile oldest sister, Anna, proved an apt pupil, quick to anticipate the responses her father desired; Louisa, in contrast, proved headstrong, often resisting or subverting the lessons that Bronson laboured to elicit but actually imposed. From the time they were infants, Bronson recorded the most minute details of their development in his journals, and when they were old enough to write, required that they keep journal themselves. These journals, while designed to encourage free expression, were open to their parents' scrutiny. Louisa's childhood journals reveal a moving dialogue with her mother, for Abigail Alcott, sharing Louisa's passionate nature, tried gently to modify it. Time and again, Louisa resolves to be good, i.e. self-denying, or repents having been bad, i. e. selfish or angry.

Life was further complicated for Louisa, as for the entire family, by their poverty. When Bronson's Temple School failed, he abdicated from his responsibility as breadwinner. Living primarily on the largess of his friend Ralph Waldo Emerson and his wife's relatives, Bronson retired to Concord, from which he issued 'Orphic Sayings'. The family's darkest hours were spent at Fruitlands, an experiment in communal living that Bronson launched with the help of an English friend, Charles Lane. Here Bronson, Lane, and other friends philosophised and strove to purify themselves, while Abigail and her daughters attempted to wrest a meagre subsistence from the soil. Exhausted in mind and body, Abigail threatened to leave her husband, who then fell into a severe depression. At last the family returned intact to Concord and the patronage of Emerson. As a result of this experience eleven-year-old Louisa determined to become economically self-sufficient and to provide her mother with the comforts that Bronson could or would not.

Back in Concord, Louisa enjoyed the society of the Emersons, the Nathaniel Hawthornes, and Henry David Thoreau. She began writing and, with the help of Anna, staging her own plays. True to her resolve, Louisa also began contributing to the family's support. She worked at a succession of odd jobs – as governess, companion, seamstress, and even domestic servant. And she succeeded in selling a few poems and stories. The Civil War proved both a curse and a boon: during her brief stint as army nurse, Louisa contracted an illness that was to impair her health permanently; yet her account of that experience, *Hospital Sketches* (1863), brought her recognition and later the invitation from Roberts Brothers to write for them a 'girls' book'.

During her years of literary apprenticeship, Alcott witnessed the marriage of her sister Anna, the death of her sister Elizabeth, and the growing determination of her sister May to become an artist. She published one novel, *Moods* (1865), the story of a misguided and

broken marriage, but at the instigation of her publishers she omitted
ten chapters. Whether owing to this omission or to its daring theme,
the book met with mixed reviews. She laboured at a largely autobiographical second novel, 'Success' (later published as *Work*), while
effortlessly producing the sensation stories that she professed to
regard as 'rubbishy tales'.[5] Rediscovered and highly regarded by
feminist scholars, Alcott's adult works have prompted re-evaluation
of *Little Women*, her children's classic.[6]

Several critics see Jean Muir, the fortune-hunting actress turned
governess of *Behind a Mask*, as anticipating Alcott's transformation
from sensation story writer into a purveyor of 'moral pap for the
young'.[7] More obvious precursors of *Little Women* are the early story
'A Modern Cinderella' (1860) and 'Psyche's Art' (1868), published
the same month that Alcott was approached by Roberts Brothers.[8]
Both Stories, like *Little Women*, are based on the experience of Alcott
and her sisters. *Little Women* of course contains portraits of all four
Alcotts: Meg March, like Anna, is domestic, Jo, like Louisa, is a
tomboy and writer; Beth, like Elizabeth, is frail and dies; and Amy,
like May, is charming and artistic. 'A Modern Cinderella' seems to
have been written in tribute to Anna Alcott, for the self-centred
literary and artistic sisters, Diana and Laura, are subordinated to
Nan, called 'little woman' and 'Martha' by her father and 'my "angel
in the house"' by the hero, modelled on Anna's husband John Pratt.
'Psyche's Art' was perhaps designed as a similar tribute to May
Alcott, though her name is given to the dying sister of the heroine,
who is called Psyche, Bronson's name for Elizabeth. Although the
number of sisters varies in these stories from two to four, certain
elements remain constant: in each, a sister (Beth, Nan, Psyche) sacrifices her own interests to those of the family; in each, one or more
sisters (Jo, Diana and Laura, Psyche) learns to put 'that humble and
more human teacher, Duty' before 'the goddess Beauty';[9] in each a
sister (Beth, Nan, May) sickens, Nan and Beth as a result of their
sacrifices. Finally, as the artists and writers learn to subordinate their
needs to those of their families, their art becomes less heroic and
ambitious, more domestic and humble: Diana resolves to 'turn my
books and pen to some account, and write stories of dear old souls
like you [the hero] and Nan' (p. 292); Jo likewise writes homely
stories about ordinary people and, like Psyche, whose sister also
dies, resumes her art at the urging of her family, finding in it solace
for her grief. The lesson of these female artists, then, appears to be
the lesson that Alcott supposedly learned: to subordinate their needs

for artistic expression to the needs of their families and to use their artistic talents for the benefit not only of their own families but of the family as an institution.[10]

But though Alcott provided family entertainment by fictionalising and thus supporting her own family, her view of families in *Little Women* is complex and disturbing.[11] In her Preface Alcott instructs her 'little book' to 'show to all / That entertain, and bid thee welcome shall,/What thou dost keep close shut up in thy breast'. What we find are cosy scenes and sweet sermons but also the self-inflicted wounds that are a women's price of membership in the patriarchal family.[12] From the famous opening 'Christmas won't be Christmas without any presents', the March girls engage in self-sacrifice. Prompted by Marmee's belief that 'we ought not to spend money for pleasure, when our men are suffering so in the army' (p. 7), the girls forgo Christmas presents for themselves in order to purchase gifts for their mother. Later in the chapter they receive a letter from their absent father, a Union Army chaplain, exhorting them to 'fight their bosom enemies bravely and conquer themselves so beautifully that when I come back to them I may be fonder and prouder than ever of my little women' (p. 16). Amy's response – 'I *am* a selfish pig! but I'll truly try to be better' – is simply the most vehement expression of what they all feel. Marmee then recommends that they play in earnest their childhood game of Pilgrim's Progress and 'see how far on you can get before Father comes home' (p. 18). Women's pilgrimage, Alcott implies, is merely a game, an imitation of men's, and it takes place within the confines of the home for the purpose of winning male approval.

Little Women abounds in images of constriction, concealment, and pain. Early in the book Meg and Jo attend a party. Because Jo has soiled her gloves, and because, according to Meg, 'a real lady is always known by neat boots, gloves, and handkerchief' (p. 37), she must force her hand into a glove of Meg's. Worse, Jo has scorched her dress by standing too close to the fire and thus must keep her back to the wall in order to conceal the damage – or the damaging truth of her own fiery nature. Meg, whose 'tight slippers tripped about so briskly that none would have guessed the pain their wearer suffered smilingly' (p. 38), pays for her dubious pleasure with a sprained ankle. Jo meanwhile experiences exhilaration when she meets Laurie, forgets the need to conceal her dress, and dances a spirited polka in the privacy of the hall. But Meg's accident soon recalls her to her 'blundering' self. This chapter, in which Meg gladly

Elizabeth Lennox Keyser

suffers while Jo briefly escapes only to be confined again within the uncomfortable role of little woman, anticipates the course their lives will take.

Meg, on later accepting the proposal of Laurie's tutor John Brooke, is described as 'enthroned upon his knee and wearing an expression of the most abject submission' (p. 286). This image conveys the illusory sense of power that courtship confers upon women and the perpetual childhood to which marriage dooms them. Meg's marriage, as described in Part Two (originally entitled *Good Wives*), exemplifies the constrictions – physical, mental, and emotional – to which even Jo finally adapts. The lawn of Meg's home, which she calls 'my baby-house', is 'about as big as a pocket-handkerchief', and her dining room is described as a 'tight fit' (pp. 300, 297). Just as Meg earlier had to smile though her slippers pinched her feet, so now she must gracefully, even gratefully, accept her cramped and narrow lot in life. In the one quarrel we witness between Meg and John, she declares, 'I'm sick, dead – anything' (p. 343). Rash as these words are, the imagery surrounding Meg's marriage suggests a living death. After the birth of her twins, Daisy and Demi, Meg complains to Marmee that she is 'on the shelf'. Marmee, to do her justice, exhorts Meg not to 'shut yourself up in a bandbox because you are a woman, but understand what is going on, and educate yourself to take your part in the world's work' (p. 482). Eventually, however, Meg learns 'that a woman's happiest kingdom is home' – 'the sort of shelf on which young wives and mothers may consent to be laid, safe from the restless fret and fever of the world, finding loyal lovers in the little sons and daughters who cling to them' (p. 491). The image of the shelf, the passive verb 'laid', and the idea that children are the most appropriate lovers for adult women all imply that marriage arrests female development. Just as the title of Part One, 'Little Women', suggests that adolescent girls should be miniature adults, so the extension of that title to Part Two suggests that 'good wives' should remain little women or girls.

Jo, with the help of her male alter-ego Laurie, struggles valiantly to avert a similar fate. Confined, almost imprisoned in the big house next door, Laurie is freed by Jo in a reversal of the Sleeping Beauty tale. In boldly entering the house which she regards as 'a kind of enchanted palace, full of splendors and delights', and by confronting gruff old Mr Laurence, Jo seems to be appropriating male power and freeing a part of her own nature. Laurie not only accepts, encourages, and provides a model for the development of Jo's masculine side; he also elicits and nurtures the feminine. On Jo's first visit to the 'enchanted palace', she enters like a male hero but presents herself to Laurie as a nurse. Later when Beth lies critically ill, Jo, despite her belief that 'tears were an unmanly weakness' (p. 97), allows herself to break down in Laurie's presence and be comforted by him. And though Jo's bracing companionship has tended, much to his grandfather's delight, to make him more manly, Laurie has learned, through contact with the feminine household, how to offer maternal support. In words that recall Marmee's on another occasion, he says, 'I'm here, hold on to me, Jo, dear' and silently strokes 'her bent head as her mother used to do' (p. 228). In short, the friendship of Laurie and Jo seems to provide the best of both spheres – masculine strength and freedom from sentimentality together with feminine sympathy. But in having Jo later reject Laurie's proposal of marriage (much to her contemporary readers' chagrin), Alcott indicates that in society as it was then constituted such androgynous wholeness was impossible.

Jo, unlike her sisters, consciously aspires to independence, but she internalises familial values to the point that she cannot seek it without guilt. In her own play 'The Witch's Curse', Jo unwittingly dramatises the forces arrayed against her.[13] By casting herself as both the hero and the villain, she not only plays 'male parts to her heart's content' (p. 25) but portrays her dangerous self-division. And by casting Meg as her antagonists, the 'cruel sire' and the witch herself (as well as Beth as a 'black imp'), she identifies a threat to self within the family. Jo views the publication of her first story as the initial step in realising 'the dearest wishes of her heart' – 'to be independent, and earn the praise of those she loved' (p. 194). But the two wishes, like her two male characters, are conflicting, if not incompatible: to achieve independence she will have to assert herself in such a way as to incur blame; and to win the praise of those she loves best, she will have to curtail, or at least modify, her striving for independence. When Meg is staying with the worldly Moffats, she slips Marmee's note 'into her pocket as a sort of talisman against envy, vanity, and false pride' (p. 109). Similarly, Jo pins Marmee's note inside her frock as 'a shield and reminder, lest she be taken unaware' (p. 151). Jo must guard against her emotions at all times; otherwise she will disappoint her mother and, through her, her father. When, upon his return, Mr March praises Jo, causing her to blush with pleasure, it is for having become 'a young lady who pins her collar straight, laces her boots neatly, and neither whistles, talks slang, nor lies on the rug, as she used to do' (p. 274) – that is, a lady as defined earlier by Meg.

Even when Jo leaves home, she cannot escape the strictures of her family. Encouraged by Marmee, who believes that Jo and Laurie 'are too much alike and too fond of freedom' (p. 407) to marry, Jo goes to New York where, just as she is getting a taste of independence, she finds in staid Professor Bhaer the 'something sweeter' than the freedom that Marmee had wished for her (p. 408). Described as a 'genial fire' – 'people seemed to gather about him as naturally as about a warm hearth' (p. 431), Bhaer, like Jo's parents, throws a damper on her creative powers. Just as Jo's father, when she won a cash prize for a sensation story, urged her to 'Aim at the highest, and never mind the money' (p. 332), Bhaer encourages Jo to emulate Shakespeare. But as Virginia Woolf points out in *A Room of One's Own*, women cannot write like Shakespeare until, freed from the fetish of chastity, they are allowed to experience life as he and other male writers have done.[14] Jo, under the stimulus of her sensation writing, has begun to free herself and to experience life, at least vicariously: 'as thrills could not be produced except by harrowing up the souls of the readers, history and romance, land and sea, science and art, police records and lunatic asylums, had to be ransacked for the purpose' (p. 430). As a result, Jo begins to catch 'glimpses of the tragic world which underlies society', but the narrator, like Professor Bhaer, reproves her for 'beginning to desecrate some of the womanliest attributes of a woman's character' (p. 430). Earlier Jo, to accommodate her family's suggestions for her first serious novel, had 'laid her firstborn on the table, and chopped it up as ruthlessly as any ogre' (p. 335). Now when Bhaer, in disgust, burns a sheet of the *Weekly Volcano* for which Jo writes, she rereads her work, feeling as though she is wearing 'the Professor's mental or moral spectacles' (p. 438). 'Wishing . . . that father and mother hadn't been so dread-fully particular about such things' (p. 439), Jo consigns her three months' work to the flames.

Professor Bhaer saves Jo from 'the frothy sea of sensational lit-erature' (p. 429) only to plunge her into a slough of creative and personal despond. Having sacrificed the *Weekly Volcano* and what she calls the 'vortex' of creativity to Bhaer's 'genial fire', Jo goes on to sacrifice Laurie. Her reasoning – 'You'd hate my scribbling, and I couldn't live without it' (p. 449) – seems disingenuous, for Laurie, who greeted the sale of her first story with a 'Hurrah for Miss March, the celebrated authoress!' (p. 188), has always championed her writing. In fact, Jo's writing has threatened and been threatened by those within the family or those who, like Professor Bhaer, stood *in loco parentis*. Marmee always 'looked a little anxious when "genius took to burning" ', perhaps because Jo begins 'to feel herself a power in the house' (p. 353). Amy as a child had spitefully burned Jo's first manuscript, and that wanton act anticipates the way Jo, as her parents' child, destroys her own work. Jo, in rejecting Laurie, feels much as she did when editing her work against her better judgement – 'as if she had murdered some innocent young thing and buried it under the leaves' (p. 450) – or 'as if she had stabbed her dearest friend' (p. 455). And in turning from Laurie to her dying sister, it is as though she chooses to wed death rather than life.

Beth, the only March girl incapable of imagining a life outside her parents' home, has always 'unconsciously exercised more influence than anyone in the family' (p. 54) over Jo. Now their time at the shore is described as a honeymoon: they are 'all in all to each other . . . quite unconscious of the interest they excited in those about them' (p. 457). Before returning home, Jo, with a 'silent kiss', 'dedicated herself soul and body to Beth' (p. 462) and in a poem asks Beth to 'Give me that unselfish nature' (p. 512). Gradually, Jo begins to feel 'that I won't lose you, that you'll be more to me than ever, and death can't part us'. Beth promises, 'I shall be your Beth, still' and urges Jo to take her place, assuring her, 'you'll be happier in doing that than writing splendid books or seeing the world'. In response 'then and there Jo renounced her old ambition and pledged herself to a new and better one' (p. 513). After Beth dies, Jo assumes her role: she takes shelter in her mother's arms, sits in Beth's little chair close beside her father, and wields Beth's housekeeping implements. Marmee, realising it is now safe to do so, encourages Jo to 'write something for us, and never mind the rest of the world' (p. 535). Her father mails the piece to a popular magazine where it is accepted. Jo wonders, 'What *can* there be in so simple a little story . . . to make people praise it so?' Her father tells her, 'you have found your style at last'; but Jo demurs: 'If there *is* anything good or true in what I write, it isn't mine; I owe it all to you and mother, and to Beth' (p. 535). Jo's stories now, rather than letting 'the passions have a holiday' (p. 330), are 'little stories', 'humble wanderers', received by a 'charitable world' and sending back 'comfortable tokens to their mother, like dutiful children' (pp. 535–6). The image of the female artist as mother, her works as dutiful children, and their reception as charitable suggests Jo's withdrawal into the domestic and dependent sphere from which she had sought escape.[15]

Jo is a subversive figure in so far as she expresses a woman's legitimate longing for a larger sphere of activity. But seeing no way to satisfy self, she adopts a policy of selflessness and, thus diminished, succumbs to the marriage proposal of fatherly Professor Bhaer. More subversive than Jo, and potentially the more successful artist, is Amy, for she is not afraid to assert herself, take risks, and appear selfish or foolish. As the pampered baby of the family, she does not feel the need to earn its love or fear its disapproval. Therefore, from the beginning of the book, she is the least willing to engage in self-sacrifice. When her sisters decide to spend their Christmas dollars on presents for Marmee, Amy resolves to spend but a part of hers. (She later weakens but only for the purpose of making the most impressive display!) The most worldly of the sisters, she is also the most eager to venture out into the world or, something the others never try to do, bridge the gap between world and home. Thus Amy attends school while Beth tends the house, teases to accompany the older girls on their grown-up outings, and braves their ridicule by planning a luncheon for her wealthy classmates. The only one to invite outsiders (apart from the Laurences) into the charmed family circle, Amy is removed from that circle in times of crisis. When Beth is ill, Amy stays with Aunt March; when Beth is dying, Amy remains in Europe, where she, not Jo, satisfies a lifelong ambition to study art abroad. Even Amy's marriage to Laurie takes place there rather than in the bosom of the family as Meg's does. Perhaps most significant, in the family tableaux that end both parts of *Little Women*, Amy is a figure somewhat apart, and it is she, not Jo, who is portrayed as the artist, engaged herself in portraying the family. At the end of Part One, a scene in which everyone else is paired. 'Amy was drawing the lovers' (p. 289); at the end of Part Two, Amy, albeit 'with a beautiful motherly expression on her face, sketched the various groups' (p. 598). It is as though Amy's comparative detachment from the family and its self-denying ethos frees her to record it.

Amy's subversiveness, like that of *Little Women* itself, is easy to ignore because, as in Jo's play, she appears the conventional heroine to Jo's hero. Always ladylike, Amy shrewdly defines Jo's version of independence as a desire to 'go through the world with your elbows out and your nose in the air' (p. 321). Jo's unconventionality, while genuine, is, as Amy implies, a matter of appearance and manners; she is only independent of those for whom she cares nothing. Amy, on the other hand, moderates her behaviour so as to please those who can help her, but she is truly independent of her family's judgement, as when she plans her luncheon party. Amy's early 'artistic attempts', like her social pretensions, are treated mockingly,

but these too suggest that Amy, unlike Jo, possesses true independence. For example, Amy casts her own foot and has to have it
dug out of the plaster by Jo, who 'was so overcome with laughter
while she excavated that her knife went too far' and 'cut the poor
foot' (p. 317). The image implies that Amy puts herself into her work
and that Jo, in an attempt to extricate life from art, does injury to
both. Further, at the end of a long passage that seems to disparage
Amy's art, the narrator adds that Amy 'persevered in spite of all
obstacles, failures, and discouragements, firmly believing that in
time she should do something worthy to be called "high art"'
(p. 317). Unlike Jo, Amy does not give up or modify her art in
response to criticism from her family or from those who embody its
values. Instead, she discovers on her own that 'talent isn't genius'.
As she tells Laurie, 'Rome took all the vanity out of me' (p. 498).
While Jo subjects her work to Professor Bhaer's 'moral spectacles',
Amy uses the gauge of superior work, in this case the greatest
masterpieces. Even after surrendering her ambitions, Amy continues working for her own pleasure; she does not need parental en-
couragement – or permission – to resume a proscribed activity.

Amy's courtship and marriage reflect her greater independence
but also point up its possible limitations. During their European
courtship, she is assertive: when driving with Laurie, she holds the
reins, and, unlike her sisters, who marry their tutors, she plays
Mentor to Laurie's Telemachus as well as The Prince to his Sleeping
Beauty. Laurie proposes as the two row smoothly through the water,
and the letter announcing their engagement is described as a 'duet'.
Theirs is the one joyous, seemingly egalitarian marriage in the book.
Once home, however, Amy appears to regress: Laurie calls her 'little
woman', Jo buttons her cloak as though she were a child, and
Marmee holds her on her lap 'as if being made "the baby" again'
(pp. 559–60). When we think of Meg 'enthroned' on John's knee,
then laid on the shelf, and when we think of Jo in 'Beth's little chair
close beside' her father, we have to wonder whether Amy has truly
succeeded where Jo failed. Perhaps, secure in a more mature
womanhood, she can playfully allow herself to appear the charming
juvenile that her family assumes her to be.

Jo, in the dark chapter 'All Alone', bitterly compares herself to
Amy: 'Some people seemed to get all sunshine, and some all shadow;
it was not fair, for she tried more than Amy to be good, but never got
any reward, – only disappointment, trouble, and hard work' (p. 530).
Amy, as Jo dimly recognises, manipulates the forms of little woman-

hood but rejects their self-sacrificial essence; thus she avoids the painful sacrifices incumbent upon most women. Jo resents the forms but, having long accepted their underlying principle, is unable to escape them. Later in this chapter the narrator denies that Jo become 'the heroine of a moral storybook': 'if she had been . . . she ought at this period of her life to have become quite saintly, renounced the world, and gone about doing good in a mortified bonnet, with tracts in her pocket. But you see Jo wasn't a heroine; she was only a struggling human girl, like hundreds of others' (p. 534). But this disclaimer, while ostensibly distinguishing Jo's – and normal women's – behaviour from that of morbid martyrs and ridiculous fanatics, serves rather to confound them. The narrator goes on as if to vindicate Jo's self immolation or to show how she vindicates herself:

> She had often said she wanted to do something splendid, no matter how hard; and now she had her wish, – for what could be more beautiful than to devote her life to father and mother, trying to make home as happy to them as they had to her? And, if difficulties were necessary to increase the splendor of the effort, what could be harder for a restless, ambitious girl, than to give up her own hopes, plans and desires, and cheerfully live for others? (p. 534).

But the questions need not be read as rhetorical. The first one implies that nothing could be more splendid than for Jo to repay her parents, but, if their teachings have brought her to this pass, what is she repaying them for? And even if she does owe them a debt of gratitude, could she not repay them better by making something of herself? If they have devoted themselves to her happiness, can they be happy in her sacrifice? The narrator's second question demands an answer of 'nothing', but, if so, then why should this hardship be imposed? Indeed, this second question raises the rhetorical question of the book.

An answer is that such self-immolation prepares one for marriage and the reconstitution of the family circle. Just before denying Jo's status as heroine, the narrator elaborates on her likeness to a chestnut:

> Grief is the best opener for some hearts, and Jo's was nearly ready for the bag; a little more sunshine to ripen the nut, then, not a boy's impatient shake, but a man's hand reached up to pick it gently

from the burr, and find the kernel sound and sweet. If she had suspected this, she would have shut up tight, and been more prickly than ever; fortunately she wasn't thinking about herself, so, when the time came, down she dropped. (p. 533)

It is Jo's self-forgetfulness, reflected in her newly selfless writing, that brings Professor Bhaer to her. At the end of the chapter 'All Alone', Jo, having just heard of Amy and Laurie's engagement, wanders up to the garret where genius used to burn. She peruses 'four little wooden chests in a row, each marked with its owner's name, and each filled with relics of the childhood and girlhood ended now for all' (p. 538). Moved by this burial ground of all the sisters' hopes and aspirations, Jo writes a sentimental poem that recapitulates the movement of *Little Women*. When Professor Bhaer later reveals how he has treasured the poem, Jo dismisses it as 'very bad poetry' and tears it up, but it does skilfully epitomise the character of each sister. The stanza devoted to Jo, her epitaph as it were, alludes to 'Dreams of a future never found', and 'Half-writ poems, stories wild'. The lines 'Diaries of a wilful child,/Hints of a woman early old' compress into a few words the fate of 'wilful' female children in a patriarchal society. But the lines that draw the Professor to her are doubtless the next ones: 'A woman in a lonely home,/ Hearing like a sad refrain, –/"Be worthy love, and love will come"' (p. 586). While to him they may suggest ripening, to some readers (and perhaps to the author who hastily destroys them) they suggest decay.

Not only does self-immolation prepare one for marriage; it prepares one for only the least satisfying of lives outside marriage. Spinsterhood, as the unmarried Alcott well knew, provided no sure escape from unremunerated domestic service. In fact, the prospect is so forbidding that it can hasten ripening and 'harvest time', as the final chapter is called. As Jo approaches her twenty-fifth birthday, she anticipates life as a 'literary spinster, with a pen for a spouse, a family of stories for children, and twenty years hence a morsel of fame, perhaps' (p. 540). As though to correct Jo's bleak vision, the narrator supplies a lengthy passage to the effect that spinsters can lead 'useful, happy' lives (p. 542). But spinsters, as described by the narrator, sound like superannuated Beths. Girls are urged to appreciate their 'many silent sacrifices of youth, health, ambition, love itself', and boys are exhorted to chivalrous regard for 'the good aunts who have not only lectured and fussed, but nursed and petted, too often without thanks' (p. 541). The word 'old' recurs throughout the passage, and the narrator ends by tacitly admitting the ineffectuality of her argument: 'Jo must have fallen asleep (as I dare say my readers have) during this little homily' (p. 542). At this point, Laurie breaks in, to enliven Jo temporarily but also to remind her of what she has lost – her youthful exuberance and spontaneity. As she tells him, 'You may be a little older in years, but I'm ever so much older in feeling, Teddy. Women always are; and this last year has been such a hard one, that I feel forty' (p. 547). Little wonder, then, that Jo, so ripened, drops at once into the matrimonial bag extended by Professor Bhaer. Breaking into the family circle, Bhaer immediately wins the approval of Mr March, John Brooke, and Laurie to whom he lectures on the 'burial customs of the ancients' (p. 555). Indeed his advent spells the death of our hopes for Jo.[16]

Because Professor Bhaer represents the patriarchal values around which the March circle ultimately revolves, his marriage to Jo serves to perpetuate it and to preserves Jo's place in it. Jo, by establishing with her husband a school for boys at Plumfield, the estate that she inherits from her Aunt March, remains what Beth was – a retainer – only on a much larger scale. As Jo predicts, a strict division of labour by gender will obtain at Plumfield: 'Fritz [Bhaer] can train and teach in his own way, and Father will help him. I [like the maiden aunts?] can feed and nurse and pet and scold them; and Mother will be my standby' (p. 593). Among Bhaer's trainees is Jo herself, much as Marmee was her husband's: 'Jo made queer mistakes; but the wise Professor steered her safely into calmer waters' (p. 595) just as he earlier steered her from 'the frothy sea of sensational literature'. But Jo now finds 'the applause of her boys more satisfying than any praise of the world, – for now she told no stories except to her flock of enthusiastic admirers' (p. 597). Jo, at the end of Part I, had not wanted to look into the future for fear of seeing something sad (p. 289). Comparing the end of Part One with the end of Part Two, we can appreciate her wisdom. Not only is her literary silence sad; so too are the gender-segregated groups of the final family tableau. Although Marmee, stretching out her arms to embrace the scene, can wish no 'greater happiness' for her 'girls', Alcott has allowed us to question whether it be happiness at all. Alcott's contemporary readers were disappointed by her refusal to marry Jo to Laurie; modern readers are disappointed that Alcott, supposedly succumbing to the demands that Jo marry someone, married her to Professor Bhaer. But just this sense of disappointment, even outrage, this reluctance to accept the traditional happy ending as a happy one, attests to the subversive power of Alcott's design. Jo's paean to families not withstanding, we can see how hers conspired against her womanhood and taught her only what to make of a diminished thing.

NOTES

1. All references will be to M. Bedell (ed.), *Little Women* (New York: Modern Library, 1983).

2. *Behind a Mask: or, A Woman's Power* is one of a number of sensation stories Alcott published anonymously or pseudonymously during the 1860s and Madeleine Stern reprinted in *The Hidden Louisa May Alcott: A Collection of her Unknown Thrillers* (New York: Avenel, 1984).

3. J. Myerson, D. Shealy, and M. Stern (eds), *The Journals of Louisa May Alcott* (Boston: Little, Brown, 1989), p. 166.

4. See M. Saxton, *Louisa May: A Modern Biography of Louisa May Alcott* (New York: Avon, 1978) and M. Bedell, *The Alcotts: Biography of a Family* (New York: Clarkson M. Potter, 1980).

5. A February, 1865, journal entry reads: 'Wrote a little on poor old "Success" but being tired of novels I soon dropped it & fell back on rubbishy tales, for they pay best & I cant afford to starve on praise, when sensation stories are written in half the time & keep the family cosy' (p. 139).

6. For a review of *Little Women* scholarship, see A. B. Murphy, 'The Borders of Ethical, Erotic, and Artistic Possibilities in *Little Women*', *Signs* 15 (1990), 562–85.

7. In a 1877 journal entry, Alcott confessed to 'being tired of providing moral pap for the young' (204). For a convincing argument that Alcott, like Jean Muir, merely adopts a little womanly persona, see J. Fetterley, 'Impersonating "Little Women": The Radicalism of Alcott's *Behind a Mask*', *Women's Studies* 10 (1983), 1–14.

8. Although at first reluctant to undertake the task of writing *Little Women*, Alcott was actually well prepared to do so. As the editor of the children's magazine *Merry's Museum* and as a writer of occasional verse and fairy tales for children, she was familiar with the juvenile literary market. Her May 1868 journal entry reads: 'Father saw Mr. Niles about a fairy book. Mr. N. wants a *girls'* story, and I begin "Little Women." Marmee, Anna, and May all approve my plan. So I plod away, though I don't enjoy this sort of thing. Never liked girls or knew many, except my sisters; but our queer plays and experiences may prove interesting, though I doubt it' (pp. 165–6). M. Stern in 'Louisa Alcott, Trouper: Experiences in Theatricals, 1848–1880', *New England Quarterly* 16 (1943), 175–97, identifies an early sketch for *Little Women*. 'The Sisters' Trial' (1856). Still another is the fantasy story 'The Rose Family' (1864) in which the three oldest daughters, like the March girls, all suffer from some character flaw.

9.   A Modern Cinderella', *Hospital Sketches and Camp and Fireside Stories* (Boston: Roberts Brothers, 1869), p. 286.
10.   Still another example in *Little Women* is Amy March, who at the end of the book is modelling a bust of her frail daughter, Beth, at the urging of her husband, Laurie.
11.   Some of the following analysis has been adapted from my essay 'Alcott's Portraits of the Artist as Little Woman', *International Journal of Women's Studies* 5 (1982), 445–59.
12.   When Jean Muir literally bears *her* breast in *Behind a Mask* she reveals 'the scar of a newly healed wound' (p. 12). Later we learn that Jean inflicted it herself in order to shame the lover who has threatened to desert her into marrying her.
13.   For extended discussions of the theatre in Alcott's life and art see M. Stern's 'Louisa Alcott, Trouper', N. Auerbach's 'Afterward' to *Little Women* (Toronto: Bantam, 1983), and K. Halttunen, 'The Domestic Drama of Louisa May Alcott', *Feminist Studies* 10 (1984), 233–54. As Auerbach puts it, 'The March trilogy begins with a play; once it produces an actress, it can let "the curtain fall forever on the March family"' (p. 465).
14.   V. Woolf, *A Room of One's Own* (New York: Harcourt, n.d.), pp. 48–52. Alcott's contemporary, Elizabeth Stuart Phelps, has her heroine wonder, 'Was that what the work of women lacked? – high stimulant, rough virtues, strong vices, all the great peril and power of exuberant, exposed life?' See *The Story of Avis*, ed. C. F. Kessler (New Brunswick: Rutgers University Press, 1985), p. 79.
15.   As J. Fetterley writes in '*Little Women*: Alcott's Civil War' (*Feminist Studies* 5 [1978], 'Good writing for women is not the product of ambition or even enthusiasm, nor does it seek worldly recognition. Rather it is the product of a mind seeking solace for private pain, that scarcely knows what it is doing and that seeks only to please others and, more specifically, those few others who constitute the immediate family. Jo has gone from burning genius to a state where what she writes isn't even hers' (p. 374).
16.   Angela Estes and Kathleen Lant, in 'Dismembering the Text: The Horror of Louisa May Alcott's *Little Women*' (*Children's Literature* 17 [1989], go so far as to argue that 'having stretched the character of Jo March as far as she can on a rack fastened at one end by Jo's independent impulses and secured at the other end by her need to be a proper member of the female community of "Little women," Alcott witnesses the final snap of her experimental creation'. To disguise the failure of the experiment, Alcott replaces the 'corpse' of the 'self-celebratory Jo . . . with the self-effacing Beth' (p. 115), and it is she, not Jo, who weds Professor Bhaer.

5
The Adventure Story
DENNIS BUTTS

To strive, to seek, to find, and not to yield
Tennyson, 'Ulysses.'

My interest in Henty came from my father, Dr Elmo Zumwalt, Snr.,
of Tulare, California, who had read all of his books as a young boy in the
turn-of-the-century years. He wisely motivated me to begin reading them
at the local Tulare library when I was 10, and I voraciously devoured all
of them.

I consider that they taught me more about history than I learned from
more academic texts, and were key in motivating me for a life of adventure
when I grew up.
Admiral E.R. Zumwalt, Jr., United States Navy.[1]

At the beginning of the nineteenth century British children's books
generally took the form of didactic realistic tales of a domestic character. Whether their writers, such as Thomas Day or Maria Edgeworth,
were of a rationalist flavour, influenced by the ideas of Rousseau, or
religious, such as Sarah Trimmer and Mrs Sherwood, deeply influenced by the ideas of Evangelicanism, their stories were usually
short and serious, offering edifying advice about the conduct of life
in explicit terms.

Such tales were enormously popular. Mrs Sherwood's *The History*
of Little Henry and his Bearer is a representative example, telling the
story of a young English boy who dies at the age of eight after
converting his native servant to Christianity, and the book ends with
the firm instruction 'go, and do likewise.' Thus, when we learn that
The History of Little Henry, first published in 1814, reached its 30th
edition by 1830, the question we have to ask is not so much why
there were so few adventure stories written for children at the beginning of the nineteenth century, but how they managed to appear
in such large numbers only a few years later.

Those children who could read had always been interested in
romantic adventures, and chapbook versions of such stories as *Guy*

of Warwick had been available for many years.[2] Once children could read, taught perhaps in one of the many Sunday schools that sprang up in the last years of the eighteenth century, it was not easy to confine their reading only to the Scriptures. Defoe's *Robinson Crusoe* of 1719, and Swift's *Gulliver's Travels* in 1726 may have been intended as works about providence or politics for adults, but they were often read by children simply as exciting stories about the sea. Defoe's work, in fact, produced a whole series of imitations called *Robinsonnades* throughout Europe, including abridged children's versions, and the famous *The Swiss Family Robinson* by Johann Wyss, was first published in Zurich in 1812, and translated into English in 1814.

Walter Scott's historical romances, from the publication of *Waverley* in 1814, furthermore, demonstrated that exciting adventures need not be set on desert islands but could be just as thrilling when set in the historical past, and through the adventures of such characters as Rowena and the Black Knight in *Ivanhoe* (1820) he established the form of the historical novel. Fenimore Cooper, on the other hand, achieved great success in such stories as *The Pioneers* (1823) when he wrote about the adventures of his fellow-Americans struggling against hostile foes and the elements on the exotic frontiers of North America.

Crucially such stories appeared at the time when Britain was emerging from the Napoleonic Wars, a great naval and military power, and with a growing enthusiasm for foreign enterprise. The exploits of Clive in India and Wolfe in Quebec had whetted appetite for adventure in the eighteenth century, and the exploits of Nelson and Wellington in the wars against Napoleon had raised patriotism to great heights, so that the rise, character, and popularity of adventure stories for children can be seen both as an expression and a result of popular interest in the rise of the British Empire, which grew rapidly in the nineteenth century, especially after the wars with France.

In 1815 the British Empire as such had hardly existed. Although the West Indies provided the United Kingdom with its supply of sugar, Australia consisted only of scattered settlements on the coast and was principally regarded as a convict station. On the African continent Cape Colony was the only part inhabited by white people, and those Dutch, while three-quarters of Canada was unexplored. The only country that Britain really cared about was India, although even three-quarters of that was ruled by native princes and the remainder by the East India Company. During the nineteenth century, however, Britain expanded her possessions so much, consolidating her control over India and acquiring the whole of Burma, and huge areas of Africa including Nigeria, that the area over which Queen Victoria reigned in 1897 was four times greater than at her accession in 1837.

Improvements in communications by railways, steamships and telegraph, together with the availability of cheaper newspaper made the British public more aware of affairs overseas, and the use of reports from Special Correspondents, such as W. H. Russell of *The Times* newspaper, helped to sharpen public consciousness of the implications of such dramatic events as the Charge of the Light Brigade, the Indian Mutiny, the death of Gordon at Khartoum in 1885, and the Relief of Mafeking during the Boer War in 1900.

The explorations of Captain Cook and of Mungo Park in the eighteenth century, the wanderings of Waterton in South America, the scientific journeys of Darwin, the explorations of Livingstone in Africa, especially his dramatic encounter with Stanley in 1871, all intensified this interest in adventures in exotic places and cut deeply into the British consciousness. At a time when the economic system seemed to offer only the grim alternatives of unemployment or dreary factory-work, many people began to look overseas. As well as considering opportunities for trade and commerce with Britain's colonies, hundreds of thousands of British subjects emigrated to America, Australia, Canada and South Africa, because there seemed more scope for enterprise and individually, perhaps even adventure, there.

It is not surprising that Victorian children shared their parents' interests in the British Empire. Many from the middle class expected to have direct contact with its colonies when they left school, either through trade, through service in the army or navy, or by working as public servants. Rudyard Kipling's own school, the United Services College, at Westward Ho! in Devon, for example, was actually founded to help boys pass the Army Examination and then serve in such countries as India. Thus the interest in exotic places, in exciting exploits on land and sea, all within the hegemony of British imperialism, helped to create a climate in which boys and girls wished to read adventure stories about them, in which the heroes were young people like themselves.[3]

By the 1840s the adventure story for adults was well established through the works of Defoe, Scott and Cooper, whether as tales of the sea and shipwreck, thrilling accounts of the past, or exciting

chronicles of contemporary adventures at the frontier. But apart
from *The Swiss Family Robinson* and the occasional tale by a woman
writer, such as Barbara Hofland's *Theodore, or the Crusaders* (1821) or
Harriet Martineau's *Feats on the Fiord* (1840), there were no adventure stories written specifically for children.[4] Within a few years,
however, so many writers began to produce such tales that, although
it cannot be said that they invented the genre, they established it
firmly with such titles as *The Settlers in Canada* (1844). *The Coral Island*
(1858), *Treasure Island* (1881) and *King Solomon's Mines* (1885). Not all
of these stories deal with British imperialism directly, of course, but
their ambience of brave adventures in exotic parts, accompanied by
a strong sense of innate British superiority over all other races, is a
clear reflection of British expansion overseas in the nineteenth century, and public consciousness of it.

For the establishment of the adventure story as such as dominant
form Captain Frederick Marryat (1792–1848) was principally re-
sponsible. After a distinguished career as a naval officer, he became
an extremely successful author of such seafaring novels The *Naval
Officer* (1829) and *Mr Midshipman Easy* (1836). Then in response to a
request from his own children, he produced an accurate and realistic
Robinsonnade Masterman Ready (1841–2), a Cooper-like tale of contemporary pioneering The *Settlers in Canada* (1844), and his best book,
a historical novel about the adventures of a royalist family during
the English Civil War, *The Children of the New Forest* (1847).

Captain Mayne Reid (1818–83), after an adventurous life which
included serving in the American army in the war against Mexico,
soon followed Marryat's example with stories such as The *Desert Home*
(1851), and R. M. Ballantyne (1825–94) produced a whole series of
adventure stories, such as *Snowflakes and Sunbeams; or the Young Fur
Traders* (1856) after early years working for the Hudson's Bay
Company in Canada. W. H. G. Kingston (1814–80), the third of
Marryat's mid-nineteenth century successors, specialised in sea-
stories, such as the jaunty tales of The *Three Midshipmen* (1873) and
its sequels.[5]

Kingston was succeeded as editor of the significantly named *The
Union Jack* – a weekly paper devoted to boys' adventure stories – by
G. A. Henty (1832–1902), who became perhaps the most prolific
writer of adventure stories in the last decades of the nineteenth
century. A brave and intelligent newspaper correspondent who had
travelled widely, and covered most of the major crises in Europe
from the Crimea to the Franco-Prussian War as well as attending

various colonial enterprises, Henty began writing tales for children full-time when poor health made strenuous travelling impossible. Soon he was producing four books a year, ranging from historical works such as *With Clive in India: Or the Beginnings of Empire* (1884) and *Beric the Briton: A Story of the Roman Invasion* (1892) to stories based upon contemporary events such as *Jack Archer: A Tale of the Crimea* (1883) and *With Buller in Natal Or, A Born Leader* (1901).

Henty was enormously popular, with sales of his books estimated at 150,000 annually, and overall figures throughout the world, especially America, totalling 25 million by 1952.[6] In view of this kind of success, in the heyday of Victorian imperialism, it is not surprising that by the end of the nineteenth century almost every publishing house, Blackie, Nelson, Longman, Macmillan, Nisbet, J. F. Shaw, were eagerly providing stories for a young reading public, educated not only in the public (i. e. private) schools but also in the national state schools, after education had been made compulsory for all children by a Parliamentary Act of 1870. Even publishers such as the Religious Tract Society, originally founded in 1799 to disseminate religious works, began to publish adventure stories, serialising both Kingston and Ballantyne in its famous periodical *The Boy's Own Paper* from 1879. Another sign of this same phenomenal change in popular taste is shown by the way Reward Books, designed for school prizes and the Sunday School market, and which were religious in character at the beginning of the century, were gradually replaced by historical stories and other kinds of adventure fiction by the end.

The development of the adventure story outside Britain had been deeply influenced by English-language writers as early as Defoe, and the works of Marryat, Mayne Reid and Henty were widely reprinted in America, as well as contributing to the evolution of European traditions of adventure stories. Karl May (1842–1912), the popular German author of adventure stories, for example, had read widely in both Marryat and Fenimore Cooper.

Given the dominance and the popularity of the adventure story by the last decades of the nineteenth century, it is not surprising to find serious writers such as Robert Louis Stevenson using the form for such tales as *Treasure Island* (1883), and so directly inspiring H. Rider Haggard to write *King Solomon's Mines* (1885). A host of other writers continued the tradition into the early years of this century.[7]

*　*　*

What then were the characteristics of this literary form, the adventure story? What were its formal elements and how did writers use them?

The first and most important feature of the form is its blending of the probable with the extraordinary. The adventure story offers the reader the excitement of danger and the unexpected. But if the incidents of the story are too ordinary, they fail to excite, while if they are too extraordinary, they fail to be credible. Whatever the stories deal with, whether heroic fights or shipwrecks, the incidents have to arise naturally and in ways which maintain the confidence of the young reader. All the remarkable adventures described in *King Solomon's Mines* are carefully led up to step by step, the illusion of reality being created by Allan Quartermain's modest disclosures in the Introduction, by the scholarly footnotes about the *flora* and *fauna* of Africa, and by the hero's sober reluctance to play any self-advancing part in the search for the treasure, so that the unfolding of more and more dramatic events has been prepared for in ways that overcome the reader's sense of disbelief. 'The effect of the marvellous depends on an element of the real,' says Malcolm Cousins of Scott's *Waverley* novels, and that combination was not often forgotten by Scott's successors.[8]

This sense of probability is usually achieved by establishing the hero as a very normal and identifiable kind of person, generally a youth or young boy from a respectable, but never wealthy, home. Peter Lefroy, the hero of Kingston's *Peter the Whaler* (1851), the son of a clergyman, is fifteen years old when he goes to sea; Reuben Whitney, the hero of G. A. Henty's *A Final Reckoning: A Tale of Bush Life in Australia* (1887), is the thirteen year-old son of a miller, and Charles Crusoe, a merchant's son, is only ten years old at the beginning of Mrs Hofland's *The Young Crusoe* (1829).[9]

The young hero's main characteristic is usually his sheer normality; he is neither particularly clever nor stupid, but has plenty of spirit and common sense. There is some change in the presentation of the hero from his treatment in the first half of the century, when under the influence of Evangelicanism, he is apt to be rather pious, even in the novels of Marryat, but, though the hero is still keen to do what is right, he is portrayed in more secular terms by the time of Henty and Stevenson. What really matters is that the hero is someone young readers can identify with, like Charlie Marryat in Henty's *With Clive in India*:

He was slight in build, but his schoolfellows knew that Charlie Marryat's muscles were as firm and hard as those of any boy in the school. In all sports requiring activity and endurance rather than weight or strength he was always conspicuous. Not one in the school could compete with him in long-distance running, and when he was one of the hares there was but little chance for the hounds. He was a capital swimmer and one of the best boxers in the school. He had a reputation for being a leader in every mischievous prank; but he was honourable and manly, would scorn to shelter himself under the semblance of a lie, and was a prime favourite with his masters as well as his schoolfellows . . .[10]

The introductory stage of the story usually involves the youthful hero in a preliminary but minor crisis, which enables him to reveal his ability in some way. Frank Harrogate rescues two companions from drowning in England, before his great adventure starts overseas in Henty's *By Sheer Pluck: A Tale of the Ashanti War* (1884), and young David Balfour reveals his pluck by outwitting his mean uncle Ebenezer at the beginning of *Kidnapped*.

Usually as the result of some domestic crisis, sometimes the loss of parents or the family fortune, the young hero leaves home, and begins a long journey, perhaps to seek other relations or to earn a living elsewhere. In Marryat's *The Settlers in Canada* the Campbell family emigrate after losing their estate in Cumberland, a pattern repeated in Henty's *The Young Colonists* (1885) when the Humphreys family move to South Africa, on Mrs Humphreys' illness. It is quite common for the youthful protagonist to be an orphan like the eponymous hero of G. M. Fenn's *Nat the Naturalist: Or A Boy's Adventures in the Western Seas* (1883), or to lose his father early in the story as Dick Varley does in Ballantyne's *The Dog Crusoe* (1861). So the hero begins his journey – to restore the family fortune, to join the army, to look for a missing relative, to search for missing treasure – and in the process he encounters all kinds of dangers and difficulties, storms and shipwrecks, dangerous animals and fierce antagonists.

The settings are usually exotic, and even those stories set in Britain focus on its unfamiliar aspects such as the isolation of the New Forest or the Western Highlands of Scotland. Normally, however, the hero's quest takes him overseas, sometimes to European wars, but more often to the deserts and jungles of Africa, the snowy wastes of Canada, or even more obscure regions of South America or the Far

East. These unfamiliar and often dangerous locations, as well as giving a sense of novelty and freshness to the story, often act quasi-symbolically to reinforce the sense of obstacles against which the hero must struggle.

His journeys are not unaccompanied, however, and the hero often acquires a faithful companion, sometimes in the shape of a surrogate father such as the old servant Jacob Armitage in Marryat's *The Children of the New Forest* (1847). But often the companion is a friendly native, a Man Friday figure, who can speak the language and knows the local customs. Makarooroo has this function in Ballantyne's *The Gorilla Hunters* (1861), and Umbopo has a similar role in *King Solomon's Mines*. The young hero also often possesses some special asset almost as important as his human companion which will help him on his travels. Henty's young heroes have a remarkable gift for disguises and for picking up foreign languages easily, and Jim Hawkins's map, Dick Varley's dog in *The Dog Crusoe* (1861) and Captain Good's false teeth in *King Solomon's Mines* are similar examples of these really useful acquisitions.

As the hero undertakes his journey, all kinds of unexpected complications develop. Storms and shipwrecks threaten the Quest, while wild animals and skirmishes with natives assail travels by land. In *King Solomon's Mines*, for example, the hero has to overcome an enraged elephant, and cross the blistering desert and icy mountain-range before encountering his major opponent the bloodthirsty tyrant Twala. The narrative thus rises by a series of minor crises to the great climax, which is often a ferocious battle against powerful adversaries, such as pirates, cannibals, or a foreign army.

Normally, of course, the hero survives, but usually he does more than that, for the ending of most adventure stories shows him rewarded with substantial wealth and honours. It is not simply that the hero returns home and is warmly greeted by his family and friends, but that, having proved himself on his Quest, and discovered his real worth, this self-discovery has to be symbolised by the lavish trappings of material success. Sometimes the discovery of identity comes literally true, as David Balfour learns the truth about his father in *Kidnapped*, and Cuthbert Hartington in Henty's novel named after him (1899) is restored to his rightful inheritance. More usually, however, the hero returns home laden with great wealth as Allan Quartermain does in *King Solomon's Mines*.

Although the overt religious didacticism of early children's books is rarely found in these adventure stories, their authors did try to guide their young readers towards upholding such secular virtues as loyalty, pluck and resourcefulness, usually stressing the ideological assumption that the British possession of such qualities is unequalled, and that the British Empire was an unrivalled instrument for universal harmony and justice. Some writers indeed articulated the values of late nineteenth-century British imperialism quite emphatically, as G. A. Henty did, often prefacing his tales with a letter addressed to his readers, 'My Dear Lads,' in which he drew attention to the heroic feats of the story which followed, and which helped to create the British Empire. The Preface to *With Wolfe in Canada: or the Winning of an Empire* (1887) is a good example. Other writers are less explicit, although it is not difficult to read such stories as Rider Haggard's *King Solomon's Mines* as a parable of British colonialism.[11]

*   *   *

In their use of formulaic elements and stereotyped characters, it is clear that adventure stories owe a good deal to the structure of traditional folk- and fairy-tales in which similar patterns tend to repeat themselves. V. Propp has shown, for example, how Russian folk-tales contain many features common to West European stories, such as the English tale *Dick Whittington*, where a young hero leaves home to accomplish some great feat of courage before returning in triumph. Joseph Campbell has also shown how such stories, with their mixture of realism and the marvellous, their narration of the hero's journey as a Quest, and the frequently happy endings have elements in common with the myths and legends found in ancient Buddhist, Greek and Hindu cultures.

Campbell goes on to argue that such myths remain powerful because they express the unconscious desires and fears which underlie conscious patterns of behaviour, and Bruno Bettelheim suggests that folk- and fairy-tales have remained particularly popular with children because through them children learn to master their disappointments and fears, and to gain feelings of self-hood and self-worth. Many fairy tales, he points out, depict a hero who is not a superman but an ordinary person like the reader, who goes out into a world in which evil is omnipresent and often in the ascendancy. Any yet these stories also carry the pyschologically reassuring meaning that heroes and heroines can learn to survive in such a world, and even wring triumph out of it.[12]

Despite the realism of their surface structures, it is clear that many nineteenth-century adventure stories are based upon the formula of folk-tales. Inevitably they were transformed by Victorian interests and ideologies, as *The Coral Island*, for example, reflected contemporary attitudes towards race, but they were popular with their readers in part because they continued to satisfy some of the same human and psychological needs as the traditional tales.

The use of a narrative structure which depends upon the recurrence of formulaic elements has certain advantages which a less conventional, less consistently structured story lacks. The reader of such stories is tested and reassured psychologically by the recognition of familiar patterns of danger and security, but he also obtains aesthetic satisfaction as he or she learns to appreciate the way writers vary the expected pattern or use it to embody values or a personal vision which may be unexpected. (Thus Dickens and Hardy used many of the conventions of popular Victorian literature, notably melodrama and the rural ballad, to articulate their own disturbingly unconventional views.)

The presence of the familiar structure of the folk-tale is very clear in *Treasure Island*, for example. A preliminary section introduces the young hero Jim Hawkins, and then, after the death of his father, establishes the purpose of the Quest, and describes the preparations for the journey. The hero and his companions make their way to the appointed place, in this case literally a faraway treasure island, where, after a series of skirmishes, they achieve victory over their foes, and finally make a successful homecoming. Stevenson's story-pattern is thus the familiar one of hero, Quest, struggle and homecoming, containing the same elements as are found in many traditional tales, and offering the reader the same kinds of pyschological reassurance as are found there.

But Stevenson uses and develops these familiar elements with imagination, sophistication and seriousness. While part of the pleasure the reader experiences when reading the book for the first time is a recognition of the familiar, which brings a reassurance especially important to the young reader, at the same time Stevenon's manipulation of these elements makes them seem unfamiliar and thus disturbing. In this way by a combination of the familiar and the unfamiliar he creates some of the tensions appropriate to a reading of an adventure story.

In traditional tales, the hero usually acquires some special gift, and here Jim's discovery of the treasure-map is the equivalent of such a gift. And though the journey Jim makes from Bristol to the island, the victory over the enemy, and the journey home also stay close to the familiar pattern, Stevenson introduces various complications, such as the way the ship's crew splits between the loyal men and the pirates, and then he complicates the crisis still further through the unexpected intervention of Ben Gunn, and the removal of the treasure from its original site.

The story is also full of wonderfully imaginative touches – the Black Spot used as a deadly warning, Jim's visit to the apple barrel, the haunting voice heard among the trees, all rendered the more credible because the narrator is the truthful, rather impulsive, and yet absolutely normal young Jim Hawkins.

But what gives *Treasure Island* its great originality is the way Stevenson varies the expected pattern of faithful companions and stereotyped villains. For the faithful companions – especially Squire Trelawney and Captain Smollett – are only too fallible, the Squire erratic and indiscreet, and Captain Smollett a professional sailor who is too unbending. The pirates, on the other hand, are not stereotyped villains, for they combine vulnerability with their aggressive qualities. Indeed perhaps they are at their most dangerous exactly when they appear most vulnerable – Billy Bones with his nightmarish terrors, the blind beggar Pew, and Israel Hands above all, horribly wounded and half-drunk, and yet absolutely murderous when apparently so impotent.

The most striking variation of all that Stevenson plays upon the traditional pattern of adventure, however, is in the character of Long John Silver and Jim Hawkins's relationship with him. Silver is ostensibly the villain, but, though Jim is terrified when he first hears of the seafaring man with one leg, he immediately takes to him when they meet in Bristol, and they become – it is the greatest irony in the book – like father and son. (The good men Trelawney, Smollett and the Doctor are much less satisfactory substitutes.) But when he hides in the apple barrel Jim learns of the dark side of Silver's nature, and from then on he is generally confused. Silver is the leader of the mutineers, kills George Merry quite ruthlessly, and switches back to the loyal party again when the treasure disappears. But he also consistently looks after Jim, and is the only character in the whole book who shows any genuine warmth to him. Is he a villain? Stevenson asks. Silver can be brutal but he is also attractive and kind-hearted. Which is the real Silver?

Stevenson, brought up by strict Presbyterian parents in mid-

Victorian Edinburgh, was fully aware of its mixture of respectability and hypocrisy, its combination of prudery and wildness, but, although he rebelled against the tensions of home and of his home town, at the same time he never ceased to love his parents or the Scotland where he found it physically impossible to live. Not surprisingly, given this background of contradictions, Stevenson became preoccupied with the problems of the ambiguity and duality of man's nature, seeing it constantly shifting and changing, and all the more difficult, therefore, to come to terms with. And he explores this paradox primarily through the fluctuating relationship between Jim Hawkins and Long John Silver, although he also touches on it in other parts of the novel. The point is made quite explicit in the structure of the story, for example, in the disconcerting shift of the narrative in Parts V and VI, when Jim, one of the loyal party, goes off to sail the *Hispaniola* around the island, returns to the stockade to find that he had inadvertently joined the mutineers, and is believed by the Doctor to have done so deliberately. Even Jim's loyalty is questioned, in other words. What is good or bad? Stevenson is constantly asking, and he uses the traditional form of the adventure story, with all its opportunities for loyalty and treachery, for disguises and changes of side, to ask his questions.[13]

This use of what had become the traditional structure of the adventure story sometimes gives a book a peculiar ideological interest when the structure breaks down or seems to be in conflict with the author's overt objectives. When this happens, a story may be revealing by a coded version of experiences more about the age in which it was written than the author intended.

G. A. Henty's *With Lee in Virginia: A Story of the American Civil War* (1890) is an interesting example. The main plot tells the story of young Vincent Wingfield, the son of a Virginian plantation-owner, who becomes a scout in Lee's army during the American Civil War where he performs with a good deal of dash. But he is often impulsive and thoughtless, and has to learn in the course of the novel how to exercise more restraint and self-control.

As well as using the Civil War as the background for Vincent's story, however, Henty also uses it explicitly to defend the Confederate point of view. While not uncritical of the worst aspects of slavery, Henty basically defends it as a reasonable social system by authorial comments throughout the book. His view of negroes is that of the sentimental stereotype, and he ignores or minimises the widespread cruelty, the sexual exploitation of female slaves, and the economic basis of slavery as a whole.

But Victorian Britain was divided over the issue of slavery in America, for economic as well as philanthropic reasons, and the structure of Henty's story reveals those divisions very clearly. For the account of Vincent's adventures in *With Lee in Virginia* is paralleled by a sub-plot about slaves in ways which reflect the unease felt by Henty and Victorian Britain about slavery in America. In the very first chapter we see Vincent intervening to help a slave Dan escape an unjust beating; and in the next three chapters another slave Tony is so ill-treated that he escapes to Canada, and his wife is sold to another master as punishment. In fact, through the story of the sufferings of Dan and Tony and Tony's wife, the structure of Henty's book reveals a picture of slavery quite different from his overt view.[14]

So powerful was the tradition of the adventure story established by Marryat and his successors, that it continued even after Henty's death in 1902. Herbert Strang, a pen-name which concealed the literary activities of two men, George Herbert Ely 1866–1958) and James L'Estrange (1867–1947), followed Henty with such historical tales as *With Drake on the Spanish Main* (1907), as did F. S. Brereton (1872–1957) with such stories as *With Roberts to Candahar: A Tale of the Third Afghan War* (1907).[15] But many of Henty's successors in the first decades of the twentieth century inevitably reflect the great scientific and technological changes which were taking place. Even more startling than the invention of the telephone or the motor-car was the rapid evolution of flight from von Zeppelin's first ascent in an airship in 1900, the first flight of the Wright brothers in 1903, and Blériot's journey across the English Channel in 1909. The First World War accelerated the development of aviation even more rapidly, with the advent of airship and aeroplane attacks, bombing raids, and the emergence of such flying heroes as Billy Bishop and von Richthofen.

The writer who reflected these developments most clearly was P. F. C. Westerman (1876–1959), for his first books, such as *A Lad of Grit* (1908) were historical tales written in the vein of Henty, and often published by Henty's old publisher Blackie. But, perhaps influenced by the fantasies of Jules Verne, Westerman soon began to introduce elements of the new technology, whether real or imaginary, into such stories as *The Flying Submarine* (1912), and soon began to produce not only more authentic stories of contemporary naval warfare but also of flying adventures in such books as *The Secret Battleplane* (1916) and *Winning his Wings: A Story of the R.A.F.* (1919). From now on flying stories became an important sub-genre of the adventure story, and, drawing especially upon the background of World War I, such writers as W. E. Johns (1893–1968) became extremely popular, with Johns, in fact, producing a whole series of tales about his pilot-hero 'Biggles', the nickname of James Bigglesworth, ranging from such stories as *The Camels are Coming* (1932) to *Biggles Sees Too Much* (1970).[16]

But the events of World Wars I and II affected more than the technical content of adventure stories. They produced even more profound changes, leading Margery Fisher, for example, to raise the possibility that the Second World War and its aftermath had rendered the traditional story obsolete.[17] The massive loss of life suffered in two world wars, eclipsing anything seen in the nineteenth century, clearly affected society's attitudes to wars in general, while after the shocks of Gallipoli, Dunkirk and Singapore many people found it increasingly difficult to rely on the invariable supremacy of British arms. The growth of international understanding, created not only by such institutions as the United Nations but also by television's revelation of the whole world as a global village, together with the liquidation of the British Empire from 1947 onwards also removed much of the imperial basis for colonial adventures, while a fuller and more open discussion of the historical past has also made it difficult to think of all heroes as flawless and all villains as consistently evil. The ideology of a self-confident British imperialism which had underpinned the rise of the nineteenth-century adventure story eroded away, and its replacement by a troubled, democratic humanism sought new forms of literary expression.

From the 1930s some writers had found it impossible to produce stories with quite the same formulaic confidence as their Victorian predecessors. Geoffrey Trease, for example, in his historical tale, *Bows Against the Barons* (1934) wrote more pessimistically about Merrie England than his predecessors, and portrayed Robin Hood's battles against the aristocracy as tragically doomed. At the same time Arthur Ransome (1884–1967) revitalised the realistic adventure story by writing about the adventures ordinary middle-class children might legitimately experience, especially when sailing boats, in such books as *Swallows and Amazons* (1930) and *We Didn't Mean to Go to Sea* (1937).[18]

From the 1950s the historical story took on a new lease of life, perhaps inspired by Trease's pioneer work, although it is probably true to say that the form had never lost its popularity from the days of Marryat, nor declined in quality quite so steeply as the other sub-genres of the adventure story. Gillian Avery, Hester Burton, Leon

Garfield, Cynthia Harnett, Kathleen Peyton and Rosemary Sutcliff, among others, began to produce interesting work, although often taking quite different perspectives from historical writers of the past, dealing with outcasts and underdogs, for example, as Rosemary Sutcliff chooses a cripple Drem as her boy-hero in *Warrior Scarlet* (1958), or Leon Garfield portrays the life of an eighteenth-century pickpocket in *Smith*.[19]

The tradition of realistic contemporary adventure stories also changed dramatically from World War II, for when total war involves children and women at home, as well as men at the front, children are just as likely to become involved in dangerous adventures. Ian Serraillier's *The Silver Sword* (1956), about the adventures of a group of Polish children in war-torn Europe, pointed the way, and Robert Westall's *The Machine Gunners* (1975), told the story of a gang of boys' involvement with a crashed German pilot, to probe the nature of patriotism and loyalty. As society has changed and literature has begun to deal with sex and violence more explicitly than in the past, so too have children's books, perhaps narrowing the gap between them and adult books in these ways. Writers such as Bernard Ashley and Jan Needle have dealt with racism in their stories, and children's writers have also begun to deal with such contemporary issues as terrorism. In *The Seventh Raven* (1981), for example, Peter Dickinson describes a terrorist plot to kidnap the young son of a South American ambassador from the performance of an opera staged in London. But we hear the reasons the terrorists give for their actions as well as the reactions of their victims in the course of the story, and by the end we are left with some uncomfortable questions unanswered. For many modern adventure stories, instead of asserting traditional values, as Henty or even W. E. Johns once did, now present their readers with questions and ambiguities, and allow the existence of different points of view.

Similarly, in the third category of the modern adventure story, alongside the contemporary tale and the historical novel, where the flying story replaced the sea story, and the flying story has now developed into accounts of space travel and of the future, there are no easy answers. Although the use of the romance formula with a young hero and the successful accomplishment of a dangerous Quest has largely been replaced elsewhere in contemporary fiction – except in such popular films as *Raiders of the Lost Ark* (Stephen Spielberg, 1981), – with an increasing social realism and psychological doubt, many science fiction stories retain the formal elements of the tradi-

tional tale, but use them to ask questions which often remain un-
solved.

Many science fiction stories, in fact, while apparently dealing with
societies and civilisations of the future, such as John Christopher's
The White Mountains (1967) or Robert Westall's *Future Track 5* (1983)
offer what is really a critique of the way we live now, and engage
with such issues as the needs of the individual as against the welfare
of the community, or the advantages and disadvantages of the new
technology. Their conclusions are not always very cheerful, and the
individual is sometimes defeated by the conformist pressures of an
Orwellian society, or has to run away to survive, as Isaac, Jan Mark's
hero, does in her story *The Ennead* (1978).

In *Ring-Rise Ring-Set* (1982), to give another example, of children's
recent science fiction, Monica Hughes writes about the dangers and
the dilemmas faced by Liza, a young Canadian girl, as her technological society struggles desperately to deal with the return of a new
ice-age, and the outcome is still in doubt as the story ends. Where the
nineteenth-century adventure story articulated the self-confident
beliefs of Victorian entrepreneurs and imperialists, in fact, many
modern adventure stories are riddled with doubts and anxieties
about nuclear disasters, pollution, the loss of natural resources. When
western society at large is debating the future of our planet, it is not
surprising to find many children's books reflecting these concerns.[20]

NOTES

1.   Christopher Ricks, *The Poems of Tennyson*, (London: Longman, Norton,
     1972), p. 566; *The Henty Society Bulletin*, vol. II, no. 14, (Cheltenham,
     1980), p. 2.
2.   Victor E. Neuburg, *Popular Literature: a History and Guide. From the
     beginning of printing to the year 1897*, (Harmondsworth: Penguin, 1977),
     pp. 102–[122].
3.   For accounts of the British Empire, see George Bennett (ed.), *The
     Concept of Empire, Burke to Attlee 1774–1947*, (London: A. & C. Black,
     1953); John Bowle, *The Imperial Achievement: The Rise and Transforma-
     tion of the British Empire*. (Harmondsworth: Penguin, 1977); Colin
     Cross, *The Fall of the British Empire 1918–1968*, (London: Hodder &
     Stoughton, 1968); and Ronald Robinson et al., *Africa and the Victorians:
     the official mind of Victorianism*, (London: Macmillan, 1965).
        For discussion of the connections between Imperialism and chil-
     dren's literature, see especially Patrick Dunae, 'Boys' literature and
     the idea of empire, 1870–1914', *Victorian Studies*, 24, (Bloomington:

Indiana University, 1980), pp. [105]–121; Martin Green, *Dreams of Adventure, Deeds of Empire*, (London: Routledge & Kegan Paul, 1980); Patrick Howarth, *Play Up and Play with Game: the Heroes of Popular Fiction*. (London: Eyre Methuen, 1973); Jeffrey Richards, (ed.), *Imperialism and Juvenile Literature*, (Manchester: Manchester University Press, 1989); and Alan Sandison, *The Wheel of Empire: a Study of the Imperial Idea in some Late Nineteenth and Early Twentieth-Century Fiction*, (London: Macmillan, 1967).

4. Barbara Hofland, *Theodore, or the Crusaders. A Tale for Youth*, (London: John Harris, 1821); Harriet Martineau, *Feats on the Fiord, The Playfellow* (London: Charles Knight, 1841). For further details about Captain Marryat's *The Settlers in Canada*, R. M. Ballantyne's *The Coral Island*, and R. L. Stevenson's *Treasure Island*, see the references below. For H. Rider Haggard's *King Solomon's Mines*, see D. S. Higgins, *Rider Haggard: The Great Storyteller*, (London: Cassell, 1981).

5. See M. R. Kingsford, *The Life, Work and Influence of William Henry Giles Kingston*, (Toronto: Ryerson Press, 1947); Eric Quayle, *Ballantyne the Brave: a Victorian Writer and His Family*, (London: Rupert Hart-Davis, 1967); Joan Steele, *Captain Mayne Reid*, (Boston: Twayne, 1978); and Oliver Warner, *Captain Marryat: a Rediscovery*, (London: Constable, 1953).

6. W. G. Blackie, quoted in R. L. Dartt, *G. A. Henty. A Bibliography*, (New Jersey: Dar-Web, 1971), p.v. See also Guy Arnold, *Held Fast for England: G. A. Henty Imperialist Boys' Writer*, (London: Hamish Hamilton, 1980).

7. For more detailed accounts of the rise of the adventure story, see B. Alderson (ed.), F. J. Harvey Darton's *Children's Books in England: five centuries of social life*, third edition revised. (Cambridge: Cambridge University Press, 1982); G. Avery, *Nineteenth Century Children*, (London: Hodder & Stoughton, 1965); and J. S. Bratton, *The impact of Victorian Children's Fiction*, (London: Croom Helm, 1981). The connections between education, publishing and children's reading are also discussed by R. D. Altick, *The English Common Reader*, (Chicago: University of Chicago Press, 1957). For accounts of the rise of the American adventure story, see, *inter alia*, Alice M. Jordan, *From Rollo to Tom Sawyer and Other Papers*, (Boston: Horn Book, 1948) and Sally Allen McNeil, 'American Children's Literature, 1880–Present' in Joseph M. Hawes and N. Ray Hiner (eds), *American Childhood: a Research Guide and Historical Handbook*, (Westport, Conn.: Greenwood, 1985). There is a useful account of the rise of the German adventure story in Kevin Carpenter and Bernd Steinbrink, *Ausbruch und Abenteuer: Deutsche und englische Abenteuerliteratur von Robinson bis Winnetou*, (University of Oldenburg, 1984).

8. M.J. Cousins, *The Adventure Story in the Nineteenth Century*, a dissertation submitted in fulfilment of the requirements for the degree of Master of Arts in the University of Birmingham, (Birmingham, 1967), p. 4.

9. Barbara Hofland, *The Young Crusoe or the Shipwrecked Boy*, (London: A.K. Newman, 1829). For further details about *Peter the Whaler* and *A*

82 *Dennis Butts*

Final Reckoning, see M. R. Kingsford and R. L. Dartt, *notes 5 and 6 above*.

10. G. A. Henty, *With Clive in India, Or, The Beginning of an Empire*, (London: Blackie, n.d.), p.11.

11. Geo, Manville Fenn, *Nat the Naturalist: or a Boy's Adventures in the Eastern Seas*, (London: Blackie, 1883); R. L. Stevenson, *Kidnapped being Memoirs of the Adventures of David Balfour in the Year 1751*, (London: Cassell, 1886). For further details about *By Sheer Pluck, Cuthbert Hartington's Adventures, With Wolfe in Canada* and *The Young Colonists*, see R. L. Dartt, *op. cit.*; for further details about *The Gorilla Hunters* and *The Dog Crusoe*, see E. Quayle *op. cit.*; and for details of *The Children of the New Forest* and *The Settlers in Canada*, see O. Warner, *op. cit.*

12. Bruno Bettelheim, *The Uses of Enchantment; The Meaning and Importance of Fairy Tales*, (London: Thames & Hudson, 1976); Joseph Campbell, *The Hero with a Thousand Faces*, Bollingen Series XVII, (New Jersey: Princeton University Press, 1971); V. Propp, *Morphology of the Folktale*, first edition translated by Lawrence Scott with an Introduction by S. Pirkova-Jacobson; second edition revised and edited with a Preface by Louis A. Wagner/New Introduction by Alan Dundee, (Austin: University of Texas Press, 1975).

13. For further discussion of R. L. Stevenson, see Dennis Butts, *R. L. Stevenson*, (London: Bodley Head, 1966); David Daiches, *Robert Louis Stevenson*, (Glasgow: William Maclellan, 1947).

14. See, for example, E. Halévy, *A History of the English People in the Nineteenth Century, Victorian Years 1841–1895*, incorporating 'The Age of Peel and Cobden', translated by E.I. Watkin, (New York: Barnes & Noble, 1961), p. 430. For further details about *With Lee in Virginia*, see R. L. Dartt, *op. cit.*

15. Herbert Strang, *With Drake on the Spanish Main*, (London: Hodder & Stoughton, 1907); F. S. Brereton, *With Roberts to Candahar: A Tale of the Third Afghan War*, (Blackie, London, 1907).

16. For a fuller account of the Flying Story, see Dennis Butts, 'Flying Stories 1900–1950', in Jeffrey Richards (ed.), *Imperialism and Juvenile Literature*, (Manchester: Manchester University Press, 1989), pp. 126–43.

17. Margery Fisher, The *Bright Face of Danger*, (London: Hodder & Stoughton, 1986), pp. 370–71.

18. Arthur Ransome, *Swallows and Amazons*, (London: Jonathan Cape, 1930); *We Didn't Mean to Go to Sea*, (London: Jonathan Cape, 1937); Geoffrey Trease, *Bows Against The Barons*, (London: Martin Lawrence, 1934).

19. See, for example, Gillian Avery, *A Likely Lad*, (London: Collins, 1971); Hester Burton, *Time of Trial*, (Oxford: Oxford University Press, 1964); Leon Garfield, *Smith*, (London: Constable, 1967); Cynthia Harnett, *The Wool-Pack*, (London: Methuen, 1951); K. M. Peyton, *Flambards*, (Oxford: Oxford University Press, 1967); and Rosemary Sutcliff, *Warrior Scarlet*, (Oxford: Oxford University Press, 1958).

20. Bernard Ashley, *The Trouble with Donovan Croft*, (Oxford: Oxford University Press, 1974); John Christopher, *The White Mountains*, (London:

Hamish Hamilton, 1967); Peter Dickinson, *The Seventh Raven* (London: Gollancz, 1981) and *Tulku* (London: Gollancz, 1979): Monica Hughes, *Ring-Rise Ring-Set*, (London: Julia Macrae, 1982); Jan Mark, *The Ennead*, (London: Kestrel, 1978); Jan Needle, *My Mate Shofiq*, (London: André Deutsch, 1978); Ian Seraillier *The Silver Sword*, (London: Jonathan Cape, 1956); and Robert Westall, *Future Track 5*, (London: Kestrel, 1983) and *The Machine Gunners*, (London: Macmillan, 1976).

6

Social Class and Educational Adventures: Jan Needle and the Biography of a Value

FRED INGLIS

I

From a little way off, the moral history of a human value is easy to write and generally follows one of two hearteningly simple narratives. The first one goes down. It selects a fine old value from the past and, commending it to the present, describes its painful decline to its present degradation.

The second narrative goes up. It takes its favoured value and follows it from its abused and self-deluded past through various salutory lessons to a present in which it is understood and placed for the first time. Thus, reassuringly, the errors of the past become the materials of present self-congratulation.[1]

It has been like this with, for instance, the history of sexuality until Foucault rewrote it all. The optimists were the audience to a tall tale in which the Victorians spoiled everything until by way of D. H. Lawrence and Marie Stopes perfect sexual freedom was, as Larkin tells us, restored in

> Nineteen sixty three
> (Which was rather late for me)
> Between the end of the *Chatterley* ban
> And the Beatles' first LP.[2]

The pessimists in this case told exactly the same story, but turned its ending into an unhappy one.

In the case of adventure stories and their strong cognates, heroism, manliness, courage and others, the values at their heart have largely been matched to the optimistic and unendearingly self-congratulating versions. That is to say, contemporary teachers and the novelists they approve of bend themselves to show by way of well-pointed morals and severely adorned tales that heroism, at least of the military kind which is its more conventional image, is a fatuous illusion leading to a pointless death; that manliness is a euphemism for patriarchal oppression; that valour boils down to a lack of discretion or to moral luck.[3] 'Wise up, kid' they tell the children ardent for some desperate glory. 'it's all lies'; or 'it was an accident'; or – as Monty Python used to tell us, 'it was all *silly*'. The path of glory lead heroes to the grave and a lot of people, not themselves heroic, are led there too.

On this foreshortened view of the history of a concept, Victorian high-mindedness and public school idealism led directly to the Somme where literature, at least, was jolted awake by Wilfred Owen and Robert Graves. Thereafter, as the light faded on empire, self-confident and righteous adventure fell gradually away and that unheroic but doughty fraction of the petit bourgeoisie, the school-teachers, were happy to see it go.

One sees their point, though perhaps the innumerable children of so many lands who read the most prodigal writer ever to pen adventure stories have still failed to be pierced by it. Enid Blyton still addresses children in 128 languages,[4] and *her* children are nothing if not adventurous.

But of course that is in part why she is so much disapproved-of (by me, too). She keeps in vigorous circulation the great myths of boyish manliness, of the efficacy of individual action, of the great solidarities of friendship, of the joys of spontaneous freedoms innocent of all authority except a silent moral law.

Enid Blyton still speaks for this stuff and its undoubted power to stir across nations and, by now, over two generations. But the teeth of the cultural elite and its appointed task-formers have been set on edge by the same values these many years.

Let us say they were at their purest in the hands of such a mixed bunch of worthies as R. M. Ballantyne, Rudyard Kipling and Robert Louis Stevenson. In *Coral Island* Ballantyne prefigured that perfect fit of role and value which can issue in unreflective, accurate action. Given their predicament, the boys on the island act perfectly. It is worth remembering that when R. C. Churchill[5] sought to rebut the progressive schoolteacher's perhaps facile preference for the truthfulness of *Lord of the Flies* over *Coral Island*, his historical counterexample was of a group of sturdy Methodist Polynesian boys in their teens who in truth refuted Golding by re-enacting Ballantyne when themselves shipwrecked in the 1940s.

The point Churchill missed was that such boys were able unassumingly to live in terms of a nineteenth-century Pacific. Their courage, physique and best moral models (manliness and so forth) fitted *A Pattern of Islands*. Modernity had not happened to them.

Modernity had happened a little in Kipling; or at least Machiavelli had.[6] Kim willingly takes on his role as dogsbody to the British spy while continuing as novice to the mendicant saint. But he is vaguely aware of a gap between good conduct and reasons of state. The gap is satisfactorily filled by invoking the benevolence of British imperialism in the Raj which, E. M. Forster notwithstanding, was at that date not an altogether weak link between the two.

The point is that Kipling is a good enough writer (and political thinker) to acknowledge a lack of fit, of common focus, between inner life and outer action. As this lack of fit becomes harder and harder to live with, so the seas and islands of adventure become more and more of a fantasy.

Stevenson in *Treasure Island* openly admits that reasons of state trump the virtues – that winning the treasure and defeating the enemy by any means to hand come first – and thereby he solves the difficulty of action by turning it into an economic competition, still the unproblematic value for capitalism. Of course Stevenson's masterpiece is wonderfully subtle with this parable, and undercuts the directness of its appeal by making the villainous Silver so irresistibly attractive, and Trelawney and the Doctor ruthless and class-arrogant bullies. But that is *his* modernity.

It is no privilege, this modernity. But it is, it seems, inescapable. It confers on its victims a new, self-reflecting and contradictory consciousness.[7]

II

The adventure story arose from a peculiar confluence of cultural traditions, and naturally took different forms in North America and England. In America, it was the product of Frontier resourcefulness, Puritan righteousness, and private enterprise. The cis-Atlantic version was appropriately more bookish and with a more visible class-provenance. It blended a vaguely Homeric courage (a distillation of the Iliad and Seneca), a high-spirited, yearning and objectless idealism (confected by Thomas Arnold and Dr Thring, apotheosised in Will Ladislaw), and the stern roster of duties demanded by the Imperial Services in or out of uniform.

These strong compounds were brewed into thick narrative forms capable of filling the imaginative appetite of a remarkable social mixture. They fed literate boys and girls of all classes, and intoxicated them with enough staying-power to endure the First World War until at least the battle of the Somme. They gave physical action the taste of certainty, the fragrance of a lark, the satisfaction of a quest. At either Frontier, whether the Khyber Pass or Dead Man's Gulch, they took away the thinness and unpalatability of irresolution, and provided the ample proteins of loyalty, duty and command.

Then it all changed. When Forster said that he hoped to have the courage to betray his country rather than his friends, when J. Alfred Prufrock came hesitantly forward to worry about his bald spot, it all changed. Rilke announced that henceforth, 'Nirgends, Geliebte, wird Welt sein, als innen', and the calm simplicity and beautiful courage of Hector before Troy or Julian Grenfell before Mons had gone for good.

No doubt it didn't happen so very quickly. No doubt the 'old, stable ego of character' had been corroded before 1914 by Freud's theories in Vienna and Lawrence's molten spirits in Nottingham. But Eliot, Rilke, Virginia Woolf and company are the primers in which we may read the change to modern consciousness and the end of adventure. To put it as an axiom: the idea of an adventure balances an exuberant self against purposive social meanings (both hostile and friendly).

Modern consciousness has made that self plaintive rather than boisterous. A lost but intensely feeling subjectivity is the most familiar patient in the psychiatric clinics. Secondly, it has turned the ruthlessness of procedural reason upon social meaning. Max Weber's iron cage of modern systems and managerial bureaucracy has effected the *Entzauberung* – the disenchantment – of experience and left the intense subjectivity of Romanticism without a referent. Procedural or instrumental reason has gone to work upon meaning and turned much of it, including adventure and heroism, into delusion or superstition. Thirdly (to go no further for now) modern consciousness puts all its faith in the minimal concepts of political freedom: individual rights, negative liberty (freedom to do what you like so long as you don't infringe the liberty of others to do the same), equality before the law, distributive justice.

Now the gains of this slow change are incontestable. Anyone who venerates, as I do, the enormous cultural and political achievements of the British Labour Party, its admirable contributions to British freedoms and happiness, is not going to sing an old song about the lost orders of hierarchy, the rich meanings of monarch, church and community, as destroyed by the welfare state, public communications and municipal housing. Much has been gained, much lost; that's life.

But this is an essay which intends a bit more than balancing banalities. I am looking for the point at which plausible social beliefs and the imaginative life of a society cross: the intersection of ideology and the imagination. In case my series of round assertions about the forms of modern consciousness seems a far cry from fiction written (by and large) for children, let me say that nowhere are our preferred values more visibly (if genteelly) contested nor vehemently urged upon their more or less obedient audience than in the little, glowing grottoes of children's fiction.

It is not enough repeated at earnest gatherings of students of children's fiction who are not themselves children that their subject-matter is necessarily produced, circulated and administered *by adults*, without this being an any way an infringement of children's rights. Given this condition, however, and given the excellent commitment of those producers and administrators of the fiction to their own taste and judgement, it follows that understanding the texts in hand is a matter of answering the question, what values are here being urged upon our children by means of this narrative? After all is said and done about the indeterminacy of the effects of fiction, about the self-referring and involuntarily self-subverting text, the death of the author and the invention of meaning, it remains true that our narratives are our readiest and most popular way of theorising the world, and that we mark our preferences amongst them in terms of our key distinctions of worth.

III

Consequently, the migration of the adventure story from one value-realm to another is of greater importance than can be shrugged off by *plus ça change* relativism, just as it is too complete a matter to be lamented by Tocqueville conservatives in a threnody to a better past. The old blitheness of adventure has gone, along with the imperial preference, the modestly lethal technology (no nuclear weapons), the class and national righteousness, the sheer ignorance about the world, which supported it.

But because the adults who make up stories for children, and buy and sell them also, still want boys to be boys, to be brave, a bit reckless, dauntless, heroic at a pinch, and suddenly want these things for girls as well, the novelist-for-children has to find a form of action and a character style which can live out these qualities *and* encompass the exiguous demands of modernity.

It would be a rare artistic bird indeed who could resolve all these contradictory demands in a single action. Probably the best we can expect is a novelist good enough to live through and *realise* for the readers a sufficient sense of the contrary drives at work. 'One writes out of one's moral sense,' said Lawrence, 'for the race, as it were.' Well, the race needs a few ideals to follow and even heroic lives, real or imaginary, to emulate. In the meantime, an honest writer will have to bring out the difficulties of matching modernity to a rattling good yarn.

It is only fair to pick a novelist of whom one can make serious demands, otherwise the examples simply won't stand up to the strain. I take as my example Jan Needle, strongly representative for my purposes not only because he can tell a gripping and appealing tale to such as wide range of child readers, but because he starts from a strong sense of the intrinsic value of children's needful venturesomeness, autonomy, and defiance.

He endorses, in other words, the great gains won for modern life by the claims of rights, procedural justice, equality made by all those struggling to emerge from the long human custom of immiseration and exploitation. He speaks implicitly but eloquently for solidarity – solidarity of class (in the *Grange Hill* book-of-the-serial, in the astonishing *A Fine Boy for Killing*; in *The Wild Wood*) and of common humanity against racism (in *My Mate Shofiq* and *Albeson and the Germans*). In *Piggy in the Middle* he teaches children in school that our splendid British bobbies are, mostly, psychopathic and racist bullies, and that a mere girl can say so.

Jan Needle accepts, that is to say, as I do, the great promises held out to the future by a certain local, low-key and militantly domestic British socialism. He is powerful and interesting to so many teachers because of this (whatever his appeal to the children). He shares with the best of old British progressivism that hatred of class and racial arrogance which is the other side of a genial and generous nature. An important fraction of the schoolteaching constituency keeps faith with those antique values – with the idea of the state as at once just and compassionate, with an image of community, with the resonance of mutuality – and does so at a lowering moment in world history when jeering commentators are acclaiming the death of socialism.

Needle is a very present help to such as them and me in our travails in the class- and bookroom. He expresses in the real language of men the hazards and incoherences of modernity, but brings out as well that there is nowhere else we can live. By the time he has finished, the adventure as lived from Henty to Arthur Ransome has been changed utterly and at times terribly.

Ransome's is a pertinent name, for Needle's heroic children are as much on their own as Ransome's, especially when one of them puts to sea. Arthur Ransome, let us say, wrote at the last moment at which children could live their adventures in the old purity of diction – could go to sea like Her Majesty's Britannic Navy, to the Arctic like Scott (although with a proper respect for Amundsen) and to look for treasure with Rider Haggard. Ransome's children, who shared in that splendid vision of public duty and communal faithfulness, then went to war. Patriotism went one way and its bread and wine turned thick and sour –

> What if Church and State
> Are the mob which howls at the door?

Its fate was written out by Evelyn Waugh with Guy Crouchback in Crete.

Idealism went the other way, into international socialism, and had a hard time of it. Needle is one of its heirs.

Being an internationalist, he starts by telling children bluntly of the evils of nationalism, the delusions of heroism. His police are crude racists in *Piggy in the Middle* (the piggy is a pretty young policewoman), in sympathy to the National Front thugs who attack the quiet anti-racist demonstration; they finally drive Sandra the heroine out of the force, leaving only the one decent constable Terry to keep faith. Bernard starts out a crude nationalist and racist until his mate Shofiq changes his heart, and together they stand and fight the Bobby Whitehead gang.

Their victory is a bloody one. Their loyal friend Maureen, who fought with them, has an eye put out by a flying stone. Although Needle's imagination closes on the last fight in the final act in the way of the classic adventure, he is careful to strip fights of all glamour, even of justification. They are caused by human stupidity and unreason; you can't win.

In this he sedulously follows the best modern way. That is, he refuses any link between violence and virtue; he votes for social realism and telling children how horrible and pointless battles are; he is Richard Rorty's[8] kind of liberal 'for whom cruelty is the worst thing there is'.

This is, as Michael Howard tells us,[9] a fairly recent development and still not a general one: Islam, 1991 painfully showed us, retains a place in its doctrine for the ennobling values of going to war for the Prophet. But a modern left-liberal like Needle will only do battle if he absolutely must, and this leaves adventures going wrong at the end rather than right. When the Falkland Islander children meet the young and nameless Argentinian conscript in *A Game of Soldiers*, it is a matter of life and death that each terrified party puts off warfare and sees the other as a human child.

Secondly, Needle teaches the primacy of rights, of fair treatment for each individual, even going to the DSS office with Shofiq to show the readers how badly a speechless old Bangladeshi is treated. So too with that hard-to-bear stereotype of the claimants' union, the social worker stooge who comes to take Albeson to school and Shofiq into care.

But this modern lesson goes hard not only with adventure stories which have never been strong on rights and justice, but also with solidarity, which Needle and his camp-followers wish very properly to rate high. It is an aporia of modernity that in stressing the individual and his or her rights and equalities among life's chances, there is a corresponding loss entailed among the values of community and co-operation.

It is a difficulty which the French Revolution put us in and the theorists have found no way out. Classical liberalism and its fearsome progeny revolutionary socialism set out on a quest for the free development of all: one solution was the state socialism so roundly ejected from its Eastern European offices in 1989. The other was Oxford Street and Fifth Avenue consumerism. Is that the best we can do?

Needle dallies with an image or two of revolution. In his most lovable book *Wild Wood* he plays (and played early) the now-familiar game of turning round a well-known work of literature (*Rosencrantz and Guildenstern Are Dead*, *Wild Sargasso Sea*) in order to see it from the back.

Wild Wood tells the tale of Toad's chauffeur in old age. A dedicated car freak (it is his avocation) he can't stand the way the rich, nonchalant Toad smashes up these lovely machines out of wealth, vanity, utter irresponsibility. The chauffeur is an honest weasel, and lives in the wood itself. An Agitator comes, a working-class, industrial, voluble and discontented stoat to rouse the peasants and proletariat (Needle's Maoist or Leninist theory is a bit unclear at this point) to take over the empty Toad Hall and live in a bit of comfort for once.

Well, we know the rest. And in old age, the old boy is gentle and cheerful and forgiving. It is a heartwarming book, and does proper honour to Kenneth Grahame.

It is, however, a lapse in Needle's modernity – a lapse all of us trying to salvage socialism by teaching our children to be both nice and good must study. For at the same time as fighting for their rights and comforts, the stoats and weasels are celebrated for their working-class solidarity. But as we have learned from the social democratic history of Europe since the early purges in Russia, Germany, and elsewhere, it is damnably hard to have both. Needle's generous heart and enlightenment head go two ways at once – towards the rich communities of proletarian resistance and their reassuringly horrible enemies; *and* towards the clean well-lighted place in which autonomous individuals exercise their individual dignity and rights.

Thus the policewoman Sandra in *Piggy in the Middle* renounces the revoltingly racist and self-protective solidarity of the cops in the excellent and reliable name of her own conscience. Thus, by contrast, at the moving end of *My Mate Shofiq* Bernard, Shofiq and Wendy go together to face the music of retribution which they know will not be just but is inevitable. In *Grange Hill* the morals go either way, all the time, as those children and ours try to sort a new history of ideas, in which, in a slogan, Kant's duty, Paine's *Rights of Man*, and D. H. Lawrence's aristocracy of the spirit negotiate for a settlement.

IV

In Needle's masterpiece, he makes his boldest effort at resolving all these contradictions. *A Fine Boy for Killing* is a small classic of the language. It also helps to kill off the adventure story. I don't know if the ancient mariner William Golding read it before launching into *his* classic sea-going trilogy ending with *Fire Down Below*, but it might help to explain his taking refuge in dazzling pastiche from the intolerable moral puzzles of the day, if so.

Needle's novel is both fable and piece of history, *histoire* and *conte*.[10] It is set, at about the time of the 1794 Spithead mutinies, on board a

Royal Navy man o'war bound on a secret mission to the Antipodes. The captain is a monster of sadism but, as Grey Derring's researches[11] into naval punishment of the time show, not a caricature (however unfair it turns out that Charles Laughton was to Captain Bligh).

The Captain orders a fourteen-year-old midshipman, also his nephew, to pressgang a few extra men and the youngster picks up a bovine shepherd boy by making him drunk and a strong, courageous and upright yeoman caught in his wherry with some minor contraband. This is Jesse Broad, who with the young midshipman William is the focus of the story.

The story mounts through one incident after another of unrelieved brutality: rum, buggery, and the lash, as Winston Churchill reputedly said of the Navy in the French wars of the 1790s, and although Needle misses out the middle of the formula, he makes something unremittingly bleak but entirely gripping out of his catalogue of savagery punctuated by the details of bilges, vomit, latrines and storms no more terrible than stinking heat and dead calm.

In summary it sounds like cliché. Don't we have enough of this in the folk memory? But Needle knows and feels deeply his sea and sailing lore, loves it all as well, and shapes a plain, solid, terse idiom in which to tell his tale.

Behind this good craftsman's prose is a driving anger and hatred at class cruelty and arrogance which he forces any halfway decent reader to share. The urgency with which we do not want Jesse Broad and Thomas Foxford to be pressed is hardly bearable. Broad himself, a convincingly fine figure and character, he makes to carry the best of Tom Paine's beliefs. When William Bentley, a chit of a lad, jets a mouthful of spit in Broad's face, Needle brings his reader to the revolutionary moment.

Broad bears the insolence in silence, after a shuddering struggle with himself. But the captain's deliberate, unremitting cruelty and hatred of the lower deck brings the other men to the inevitable moment of mutiny. The captain has the soft, loving and stupid shepherd boy tied to a spar in appalling cold. Effectually, the experience kills him. A spontaneous, ragged and wretched insurrection takes place in which Broad and another pressed civilian with a master mariner's experience take charge in order to save lives, and put the crazed captain together with the marines and seamen, who out of sheer consternation did not mutiny, off in a long boat. William Bentley, badly wounded, remains on board.

In the desperate epilogue, Broad can barely hold the order of the ship together. But he tenderly, forgivingly, nurses William back from death's door, and in long conversations shows the boy the very best of the Enlightenment values which led on to the best of modernity. He cuts through the patriotic cant about the useless war: he speaks French and loves France. He can plainly see the stupidity of class which made the captain so mindlessly brutal and almost turned the boy into a monster. He understands how the dreadful life makes ordinary, dumb men into the scum William believes them to be. He speaks for justice and equality.

And, of course, is caught by ruling class revenge and hanged.

Jesse Broad could not go to his death unaided, try as he might. He stood between two seamen, his legs like dolls' legs, his crippled shoulder hunched. He fought desperately to stay upright on his own, but he could not. He had to be held. Even his head had to be lifted up so that the nose could be slipped over it. It was then his eyes met William Bentley's.

They stared at each other for what appeared to be eternity. As if there was no one else on board, as if they were utterly alone. They stared and stared, their faces clenched and rigid. It was like an age.

Then Jesse Broad's feet swung out and upwards with a jerk. His eyes met Bentley's just once more, and they were bulging, filled with pressured blood. Then away, high up in the air he flew, twitching on his rope. The sightless eyes, bulging out obscenely, passed across the island as he turned, then seemed to scan Spithead. Then the Gosport shore, the hill, and then he spun round back again.

William Bentley swears to the bottom of his little soul that he will testify on behalf of this noble man, save his life, and bring his hideous uncle down. His family prevent him. He is never called to the trial.

There is something in the novel of the force and simplicity – the caricature, also – of Eisenstein's *Battleship Potemkin*. But the calm tone and moral fervour, the love of the sea and the clear exposition of sailing culture and art, come together in a way which goes well beyond propaganda.

The ship restores the propinquity and comradeliness which modernity lacks. It throws abominable class exploitation into sharp relief. The work at its best is rich and resonant: it creates identity. Jesse Broad is the internationalist hero of the future. His goodness and manliness teach the boy William how to go into that future with these so hard-won historical gains. Shocking, anger-creating defeat will be turned, one day, into generous victory.

Maybe I overpraise the book a little. But it is a rare thing for a children's novelist to try to teach politics so directly and with such idealism. Then the idealism is exactly our problem. For the moral-political lessons hold much more plainly in 1794 than two hundred years later. Needle is much too intelligent, as his fable brings out, to *commend* mutiny: as I said, he goes beyond *Potemkin*. He implies reconciliation where Marxism so stoked itself up on a doctrine of vengefulness and terror. But the sailing which is the occasion for communal art and culture is now become the leisure culture of the class enemy down at the marina. Post-Fordist industrialisation prevents both identity-formation and solidarity at work. At the same time the great gains in individual rights make Captain Swift's kind of class cruelty impossible to enforce. Nobody (in Europe at least) has to bear that kind of thing any longer. The local class war is over.

V

Are we left, therefore, with Jan Needle as an anachronism? I realise of course that I have treated him in a crudely foreshortening way as a dominie rather than a children's novelist. But I do so, as I said, in order to honour the political purpose to teach children strong ideals and meanings at a time when these are so scarce and spectre-thin.

As he and I find, however, it is an exiguous business. Our best political past, as lived by a man like Jesse Broad, can find no present embodiment, and our best political present, glowing for a moment in the lives of the policewoman Sandra or the tough little Anglo-Pakistani Shofiq, is a poor bare thing, short of friends and without a job. Old socialism or new consumerism. It's a lousy choice, and no adventure, either way.

NOTES

1. Alasdair MacIntyre's point in his classic introduction, on which this paper greatly relies, to his *A Short History of Ethics* (London: Routledge & Kegan Paul, 1967), pp. 1–4.
2. Philip Larkin, *Collected Poems* (London: Faber & Faber, 1989), p. 167.

3.   Bernard Williams's idea; see the title essay in his *Moral Luck* (Cambridge: Cambridge University Press, 1980).
4.   The startling figure is given in the authorised biography by Barbara Stoney, *Enid Blyton* (London: Hodder & Stoughton, 1974).
5.   See R. C. Churchill in his brief paper entitled 'Golding or Ballantyne: Who Was Right?' *Use of English*, vol 27. no. 2.
6.   See Machiavelli's *Discourses on Livy*, B. Crick, ed. (Harmondsworth: Penguin, 1968), pp. 221–30.
7.   Much in what follows is taken from Charles Taylor, *Sources of the Self*, (Cambridge, Mass.: Harvard University Press, 1989), especially the final section.
8.   In Richard Rorty, *Contingency, Irony, Solidarity* (Cambridge: Cambridge University Press, 1989), p. 141, and *passim*.
9.   In Michael Howard, *The Causes of Wars*, (London: George Allen & Unwin, 1984).
10. A distinction made by Paul Ricoeur, in his *Hermeneutics and the Human Sciences* (Cambridge: Cambridge University Press, 1981); see the essay there entitled 'Narrative and History'.
11. Greg Derring, Institute for Advanced Studies, Princeton: Princeton University Mimeo.

The works by Jan Needle referred to in his essay are:

Albeson and the Germans, (1977), André Deutsch.
My Mate Shofiq (1978), André Deutsch.
A Fine Boy for Killing, (1979), André Deutsch.
Wild Wood, (1981), André Deutsch.
Great Days at Grange Hill, (introduction Phil Redmond) (1984), André Deutsch.
A Game of Soldiers, (1985), André Deutsch.

7
Fantasy

C.W. SULLIVAN III

In a great many respects, fantasy literature is a nineteenth- and
twentieth-century concept and creation. To some extent, publishers
and booksellers have made it a category so that readers can go
directly to the fantasy section of W. H. Smith's or Waldenbooks'
shelves and make their selections. But fantasy literature, as an international genre, developed in response to realistic fiction, a genre
only a century or so older than fantasy and itself a development of
the seventeenth-century's interest in non-fiction prose – journalism,
essay, history, and biography. Before the consciously realistic fiction
of the eighteenth century, the *Beowulf* poet, the *Gawain* poet, Shakespeare, and Spenser (to name but the most prominent) could use
what we would now call elements of the fantastic without anyone's
remarking on them as such.

Lin Carter's argument, in *Imaginary Worlds*, that fantasy has been
around since epic, saga, and myth suggests either a desperate attempt
to provide a noble heritage for modern fantasy or a sincere mis-
understanding of what modern fantasy actually is.[1] Certainly, some
of the elements of epic, saga, and myth – as well as legend and
folktale – appear in modern fantasies, but the contemporary fantasy
writer's borrowing of materials from medieval and ancient literatures for his modern text automatically makes those older narratives
no more fantasy than it makes them modern. While we, as modern
readers might consider *Beowulf* or *Sir Gawain and the Green Knight*
pieces of fantastic literature, we have no way of knowing exactly
how the original composers of or audiences for those poems felt
about them.

Reality and fantasy are terms which we use today without much
analytical thought, perhaps because, when we apply them to literature, we use them as labels more often than we use them as critical
tools. Moreover, we have set them up as opposites when, following
Kathryn Hume's lead in *Fantasy and Mimesis*, we might better see
them as separate ends of a continuum. Hume suggests that:

literature is the product of two impulses. These are *mimesis*, felt
as the desire to imitate, to describe events, people, and objects
with such verisimilitude that others can share your experience;
and *fantasy*, the desire to change givens and alter reality – out
of boredom, play, vision, longing for something lacking, or need
for metaphoric images that will bypass the audience's verbal
defenses.[2]

All literature, then, is part mimetic and part fantastic, with what we
call realistic fiction toward one end of the spectrum and what we call
fantasy fiction at the other.

'Fantasy,' Hume continues, '*is any departure from consensus reality*'
(italics in original).[3] Consensus reality includes that which most of
the population of a culture group believes to be or will accept as real.

Moreover, since the Renaissance and especially since the seven-
teenth century in England, which saw the promulgation of Francis
Bacon's scientific method and the founding of the Royal Society, the
real and the not-real (or fantastic) have been mutually exclusive
terms, and western Europeans and Americans have been led to
believe that they can know what is real and what is not. Therefore,
fantasy must contain a large element of what is not real; fantasy
must deal with the impossible.

In fact, 'impossible' is a word which appears in a good many
twentieth-century definitions of fantasy. In *An Experiment in Criticism*, C. S. Lewis defines fantasy as 'any narrative that deals with
impossibles and preternaturals.'[4] S. C. Fredericks calls fantasy 'the
literature of the impossible' in 'Problems of Fantasy'.[5] Colin Manlove,
in *Modern Fantasy: Five Studies*, suggests that 'a substantial and
irreducible element of supernatural or impossible worlds, beings, or
objects' is essential to fantasy; and he explains 'supernatural or
impossible' as 'of another order of reality from that in which we exist
and form our notions of possibility'.[6] And in *The Fantastic in Literature*, Eric Rabkin says of fantasy that 'its polar opposite is Reality'.[7]
These definitions, and others, have led Gary K. Wolfe, in 'The
Encounter with Fantasy', to assert that the 'criterion of the impossible . . . may indeed be the first principle generally agreed upon for
the study of fantasy'.[8]

The writer cannot merely toss a few 'impossible' characters,
creatures, items, or events into a narrative and call it a fantasy,
however; he or she must create a place in which the impossible can
exist. J. R. R. Tolkien said it best in 'On Fairy-Stories':

What really happens is that the story-maker proves a successful "sub-creator." He makes a Secondary World which your mind can enter. Inside it, what he relates is "true": it accords with the laws of that world. You therefore believe it, while you are, as it were, inside. The moment disbelief arises, the spell is broken; the magic, or rather art, has failed. You are then out in the Primary World again, looking at the little abortive Secondary World from outside.[9]

Others have since made similar comments about the Secondary World. In *Touch Magic*, Jane Yolen remarks that the 'amazing thing about fantasy is its absolute consistency'.[10] Lloyd Alexander, in "Flat-Heeled Muse," says that the muse of fantasy writers wears "very sensible shoes" and bothers writers with questions about consistency.[11] In *The Green and Burning Tree*, Eleanor Cameron says, 'It is required of [the author] that he create an inner logic for his story and that he draw boundary lines outside of which his fantasy may now wander'.[12] And Brian Attebury asserts that fantasy 'needs consistency' in *The Fantasy Tradition in America from Irving to LeGuin*.[13] In light of such remarks, it might be argued (as I have in *Welsh Celtic Myth and Modern Fantasy*) that the logically-created Secondary World is the second principle generally agreed upon for the study of fantasy.[14]

An important aspect of these two principles is that they are reader-oriented and, ultimately, dependent for their meanings upon readers who can distinguish between the possible and the impossible, the Primary World and the Secondary World. The audiences of *Beowulf* and *Sir Gawain and the Green Knight* lived in cultures whose worldview included a large component of the preternatural; their world was one of vast wilderness tracts in which anything might exist. Their world was one of magic and mystery. Modern western European/American readers live in a culture with a very small preternatural component; their world is largely explored, mapped and settled, with only a few spots in which a Bigfoot, Abominable Snowman, or Loch Ness Monster might exist. And contemporary consensus reality may, in fact, not include them either; the modern Western world is one of science and rationality.

For the modern reader, then, reality and fantasy have meanings which would not have been understood by the audience for *Beowulf* or *Sir Gawain and the Green Knight*. Although we cannot know how they might have reacted, it is doubtful that the people listening to the Beowulf poet would have said 'Impossible!' the way modern readers of those poems would. The modern reader makes categorical distinctions between the possible (real) and the impossible (not-real) and between the Primary World and the Secondary World (and is quite comfortable doing so). Thus fantasy literature, which by these definitions and limitations is fiction set in a Secondary World where the fantastic (departures from consensus reality) occurs in believable ways, is a product of the nineteenth and twentieth centuries and should be approached as such.

* * *

It has become a commonplace among social and literary historians that the Western cultural attitude toward or view of children and childhood changed early in the nineteenth century. Immediately prior to the Romantic movement, children were thought of as miniature adults, and their literature was, to a large extent, instructive without being particularly entertaining; but as the Romantic movement took hold and an emphasis on imagination, naturalness, and innocence developed, children, who were thought to possess these qualities in greater quantity and purer form than did adults, were assigned their own existence which, while still leading to adulthood, was significantly different from it.

Wordsworth's 'Intimations of Immortality from Recollections of Early Childhood' separates and, at the same time, attempts to reconcile the two states of being, the child having a higher state of spiritual perception and the adult a greater capacity to know and appreciate. This focus on children as innocently and naturally perceptive has led a number of critics, especially Stephen Prickett in *Victorian Fantasy* and Humphrey Carpenter in *Secret Gardens*, to discuss fantasy in such a way as to emphasise its connection with children (and all of their literature) and de-emphasise fantasy's connection with adult literature.

Prickett concentrates on Lewis Carroll, Charles Dickens, Charles Kingsley, Rudyard Kipling, George MacDonald, and E. Nesbit. Carpenter looks closely at Charles Kingsley, Lewis Carroll, George MacDonald, and Louisa Alcott in the first section of his book and at Richard Jeffries, Kenneth Grahame, E. Nesbit, Beatrix Potter, J. M. Barrie, and A. A. Milne in the second. All of the writers and many of their books are important in the development of fantasy, and Prickett and Carpenter mention a number of others in passing; but they also leave out some important books which, if not written specifically for children, had an important formative effect on all fantasy, including children's fantasy. Four of these works, two discussed by both Prickett and Carpenter and two virtually ignored by them, are signposts in the development of fantasy in the nineteenth century.

The first is Mary Shelley's *Frankenstein*. In part, Shelley's book belongs to the horror literature tradition, and her immediate predecessors were the Gothic writers – Matthew 'Monk' Lewis, Horace Walpole, Ann Radcliffe, William Beckford, and many other – of the late eighteenth and early nineteenth centuries. Like most of them, Shelley portrayed her contemporary world with something menacing added to it. In the Gothics, the menace was often, but not always, connected to the satanic or to ancient, non-Christian powers. *Frankenstein*, however, was also, if not primarily, a scientific fantasy or, more accurately, a scientific extrapolation. In his *Billion Year Spree*, Brian Aldiss credits Mary Shelley's *Frankenstein* as the first science fiction novel.[15]

Instead of rejecting the emerging technological world, Shelley extrapolated on it. Dr Frankenstein uses the latest in medical skill and technology to create his monster, and Shelley used her extrapolation to suggest that technological capabilities were advancing more rapidly than the moral, ethical, or philosophical perceptions needed to interpret and control them. Her horror is not based on otherworldly or satanic powers using humans for evil, but on humans using their own powers with horrific results.

Rejected by his maker, the creature turns on Frankenstein and destroys everything, especially his family and his new bride, that he holds dear.

Mary Shelley's *Frankenstein* may have been the formative influence on the sub-generic category of fantasy called science fiction, but that influence was not felt in force until the twentieth century's increased interest in science and technology made science fiction a popular literature. The world may not have been quite ready for science fiction when Shelley wrote her novel, but in just half a century, her first great successor, Jules Verne, began publishing scientifically-based extrapolations featuring technological marvels, many of which actually came into being in the next century. Three decades later, H. G. Wells would begin publishing his five 'scientific romances', novels which, more so than Verne's, used science fiction as a vehicle for social criticism. Ironically, Wells, like Shelley, is remembered much more for his monsters than his social criticism.

The next two books are closer to what one generally considers

fantasy, and both are discussed by Prickett and Carpenter. The first
is Charles Kingsley's *The Water Babies*. The main character, Tom escapes both from and to in this book. He escapes from the horrible life
of a mid-nineteenth century child chimney-sweep, which Kingsley
seems to have drawn in rather mimetically, and escapes into the
river to become a water baby who, living in the river, discovers an
essential kinship with the other river creatures. Prickett calls *The Water
Babies* a 'theological allegory'[16] and Carpenter remarks that it was
'full . . . of his personal convictions, his destructive hatred of the
wrong-headedness of children's authors, and his obsession with
maternal-sexual female figures and the purifying, regenerative power
of cold water'.[17] It is that, and more.

   The Water Babies is a serious escape novel. According to Prickett,
Kingsley, like many other Victorian fantasy writers, 'makes use of
"another world", but his underwater is essentially a part of this one
and is ready-created for him.'[18] It was this particular creation of
another world that makes Kingsley's novel important here, for as
Carpenter notes, Kingsley 'was the first writer in England, perhaps
the first in the world with the exception of Hans Andersen, to discover
that a children's book can be the perfect vehicle for an adult's most
personal and private concerns'.[19] Explained another way, Kingsley
synthesises the *story* component of literature for entertainment with
the *thematic* content of the literature for instruction, successfully
bringing the separate strands of late eighteenth- and early nineteenth-
century children's literature together in a single novel.

   The next book, George MacDonald's *The Princess and the Goblin*, is
also a synthesis and, perhaps, a religious allegory. Prickett certainly
thinks this way; he discusses MacDonald and Kingsley in the same
chapter, 'Adults in Allegory Land'.[20] And while that interpretation
has merit, Carpenter is more to the point in saying that *The Princess
and the Goblin* 'was in fact the first British children's book to make an
utterly confident, fresh use of such traditional materials as an old
fairy spinning in a tower, and a race of wicked dwarfs beneath a
mountain – or, rather, beneath the castle itself'.[21] MacDonald discovered that one can do more with the old tales than merely retell them;
they can be a fresh source of materials with which to tell a story.

   MacDonald's 'confident use of traditional materials' opened the
way for all manner of stories about elves, dwarfs, goblins, fairies,
and the like; and it did more. It set both the *pattern* and the *style* for
the fantasy novel. The pattern is that of the märchen, or magic tale,
in which an ordinary mortal (who is to be the hero) is drawn into a

magical adventure during which he or she is challenged and tested, through which he or she matures, and after which he or she returns 'home' to dispense justice, marry, and live happily ever after.[22] Curdie and the Princess do all of this, even though they have children to carry on after they die. The style MacDonald sets is the serious and sometimes almost medieval prose style of High Fantasy which never makes fun of itself or in any way suggests that what happens in the novel is fanciful or inconsequential; it is a style appropriate to actions upon which the fate of the world may depend.

The nineteenth-century novel in which the full potential of High Fantasy was first realised was William Morris's *The Wood Beyond the World*. Prickett and Carpenter mention Morris only in passing, and that seems unfortunate. Morris's effect on fantasy was profound. *The Wood Beyond the World* synthesises the best of what Kingsley and MacDonald contributed to the fantasy genre: style, theme, pattern, traditional materials, and the invented world. In fact, Lin Carter calls Morris's novel 'the first great masterpiece of the imaginary-world tradition'.[23] And it is the invented world that makes the difference.

When Golden Walter leaves Langton on Holm, he leaves the ordinary world for an imaginary Medieval world, an impossible Secondary World of the sort Tolkien would not define for another four decades. Walking on the docks one day, Walter sees a ship that seems to beckon him, and he decides to sail wherever she is going. More by instinct than plan, Walter arrives in a new land and becomes entangled with three persons he had seen several times before: a Maid, a hideous Dwarf who mistreats her, and an astoundingly beautiful woman called the Mistress who seems to control the other two. In the end, of course, Walter and the Maid marry, but the traditional adventures of the plot are carried out in a medieval world populated by characters from folktale and legend as well as from medieval history.

The Wood Beyond the World is also important as a part of many nineteenth-century authors' reaction to the new emphasis on science and technology that was central to the Industrial Revolution. That reaction was founded, to some extent, by the Romantic poets, beginning with Blake's 'dark Satanic mills' and continuing with the emphasis on nature and ruralness found in the poetry of Wordsworth *et al.* Even Shelley's *Frankenstein*, with its dire warnings about the possible dangers of misusing the 'new knowledge' was a part of this concern. But where Shelley used the context and constructs of the new technology as a part of her fiction, Morris used the Secondary

World of High Fantasy to pose an alternative, almost atechnological worldview.

These four nineteenth-century novels – *Frankenstein*, *The Water Babies*, *The Princess and the Goblin*, and *The Wood Beyond the World* – are important because they set the standards for the two major branches of fantasy popular in the twentieth century: science fiction and High Fantasy. The science fiction of Robert Heinlein, Isaac Asimov, and Arthur C. Clarke is descended directly from Mary Shelley's novel; and the fantasies of Lord Dunsany, T. H. White, C. S. Lewis, and J. R. R. Tolkien are descended from the novels of Kingsley, MacDonald and Morris. These novels establish the subject matters and the styles, the patterns and the themes, of the fantasy that is read today; and while there are more sub-genres of fantasy than the two mentioned here, they, too, have been affected by what these four authors created.

* * *

As the century turned, advances in book production were combining with advances in literacy to expand significantly the number of books and magazines available to an ever-increasing market. This market included not only a lot more books, but an even greater number of new magazines and, soon, a new kind of book, a book of smaller size, softer cover, and lower price – the paperback. Even though most children's fantasy continued to be published first (and often only) in hardback volumes, fantasy in general found its greater and more profitable home first in the magazines and later in the paperbacks.

This expanded fantasy audience has helped make children's fantasy more popular and, therefore, more possible. It has also increased the amount of fantasy being published so that there are now categories within which to discuss fantasy literature in the twentieth century. The following categories, and most of the books mentioned therein, are from Ruth Nadelman Lynn's *Fantasy Literature for Children and Young Adults: An Annotated Bibliography*, a most useful volume which not only categorises and annotates but also cross references (as many fantasy books could legitimately be placed in more than one category) hundreds of fantasy books.[24]

Several of Lynn's categories are relatively self-explanatory. 'Allegorical Fantasy and Literary Fairy Tales' includes such examples as C. S. Lewis's Narnia books and all of Hans Christian Andersen's stories respectively. 'Animal Fantasy' is split into two categories, 'Beast Tales', serious and often didactic stories about animals trying to escape human evils as in Richard Adams's *The Plague Dogs* or Robert O'Brien's *Mrs Frisby and the Rats of NIMH*, and 'Talking Animal Fantasy', lighter and anthropomorphic stories like Michael Bond's Paddington series or E. B. White's *Charlotte's Web*. 'Magic Adventure Fantasy' includes those stories of lighter tone such as P. L. Travers's *Mary Poppins*, E. Nesbit's *The Five Children* (trilogy), and Chris Van Allsberg's *Jumanji* in which ordinary people gain special powers or otherwise come into contact with magical beings, objects, or events. A lighter tone is also present in the category of 'Humorous Fantasy', examples of which are Joan Aiken's *The Wolves of Willoughby Chase* (and its sequels), Russell Hoban's *How Tom Beat Captain Najork and His Hired Sportsmen*, and Daniel Pinkwater's *The Frankenbagel Monster*.

'Ghost Fantasy' includes Lucy Boston's Green Knowe books and Eleanor Cameron's *The Court of the Stone Children*; but Lynn saves the scarier stories for the 'Witchcraft and Sorcery' category and includes John Bellairs's *The Face in the Frost*, Ray Bradbury's *Something Wicked This Way Comes*, and Diana Wynne Jones's *Fire and Hemlock* therein. 'Time Travel Fantasy', which owes its greatest debt to H. G. Wells's *The Time Machine*, includes Janet Lynn's *The Root Cellar*, Jill Paton Walsh's *A Chance Child*, and Phillipa Pearce's *Tom's Midnight Garden*. 'Toy Fantasy', as the name implies, focuses on fantasies whose main characters are toys (regardless, almost, of whatever else the fantasy contains) and include Margery Bianco's *The Velveteen Rabbit*, Carlo Collodi's *The Adventures of Pinocchio*, E. T. A. Hoffman's *The Nutcracker*, and A.A. Milne's *Winnie-the-Pooh*.

I mention these categories here to suggest the current scope of that which we call fantasy literature, literature which includes an element or elements of the impossible and which takes place in a Secondary World (which may only be this world with the added impossible). There is one other category in Lynn's book, indeed the largest category in the book by far, which includes those works which spring most readily to mind when one thinks of fantasy literature – works such as Ursula LeGuin's Earthsea trilogy, Lloyd Alexander's Prydain novels, Susan Cooper's 'Dark is Rising' series, T. H. White's *Once and Future King*, L. Frank Baum's *The Wizard of Oz*, Lewis Carroll's Alice books, J. M. Barrie's *Peter Pan*, and perhaps the best and the brightest of all, J. R. R. Tolkien's *The Hobbit* and *The Lord of the Rings*. That category is High Fantasy.

Lynn uses the term High Fantasy for this category, and although she subdivides it into 'Alternate Worlds/Histories', 'Myth Fantasy', and 'Travel to Other Worlds', she does not really define High Fantasy other than to say that such books 'involve worlds other than our own'.[25] In his generally excellent *Critical Terms for Fantasy and Science Fiction*, Gary Wolfe does little better, defining High Fantasy as 'Fantasy set in a fully imagined Secondary World . . . as opposed to Low Fantasy which concerns supernatural intrusions into the "real" world'.[26] These definitions may point in the right direction, but they are too broad to be of much use to someone who is not already familiar with the field of fantasy. For example, these definitions could allow a newcomer to include science fiction (travel to other worlds) in this category, even though more experienced readers and critics 'know' that science fiction is quite another matter.

Lynn and Wolfe define only the location of the story; neither says anything about the style or subject matter. Dainis Bisenieks comments, 'There is no pretending, as in some modern novels, that inconsequence is the rule of life; tales of Faërie are of those who walk with destiny and must be careful what they are about.'[27] As Ursula LeGuin has said:

> I think "High Fantasy" a beautiful phrase. It summarises, for me, what I value most in an imaginative work: the fact that the author takes absolutely seriously the world and the people which he has created, as seriously as Homer took the Trojan War, and Odysseus; that he plays his game with all his skill, and all his art, and all his heart. When he does that, the fantasy game becomes one of the High Games men play. Otherwise, you might as well play Monopoly.[28]

The first and perhaps most obvious indication of this seriousness lies in the writer's style. LeGuin argues, 'The style is, of course, the book. . . . If you remove the style, all you have left is a synopsis of the plot.'[29] Style is especially important in fantasy, LeGuin continues, because to 'create what Tolkien calls a "secondary universe" is to make a new world. A world where no voice has ever spoken before; where the act of speech is the act of creation. The only voice that speaks there is the creator's voice. And every word counts'.[30]

The subject matter also makes the best High Fantasy a literature of consequence and places it in the company of the epic. As I have said elsewhere, High Fantasy implies a number of concepts which make it a particular type of fantasy: 'seriousness of tone, importance of theme, characters of noble birth or lineage (secondary if not primary characters), emphasis on magic and mystery (and an almost total lack of technology and machinery as effective devices in the action), and a generally clear presentation of good and evil, right and wrong.'[31] And although it may be true of all High Fantasy, the High Fantasy written for children and young adults is, as Lloyd Alexander suggests, 'about growing up',[32] even if it does not feature a main character who ages chronologically.

More generally, High Fantasy derives much of its form and content from older literatures. The noble knights and ladies, the magicians, the quests, the raw youth who is tested throughout before he becomes hero and king, the young girl (sometimes a princess) who will become the queen, the true companions of the hero, the villains and monsters (especially the dragons), the elves and dwarfs and goblins, the castles and caverns, and the noble ideals can be traced back through Medieval Romance, and especially the Arthurian romances, to the origins of western literature in myth, legend, and folktale. Lloyd Alexander, Alan Garner, and Kenneth Morris draw on the *Mabinogi*; Rosemary Sutcliff sets much of her fiction in very realistic ancient or Roman Britain; T. H. White bases his novel on Malory's rendition of the Arthurian materials; Mary Renault rewrites the Mediterranean stories; C. S. Lewis draws on Christian, Greek, and Norse materials for the Narnia stories; and there are many more. Even those who create their own worlds – LeGuin's Earthsea, Norton's Witch World, Tolkien's Middle Earth, and others – use characters, ideas, and constructs from myth, legend, and folktales to add depth and texture to their narratives.

Tolkien is, perhaps, the ultimate example. *The Hobbit* and, more to the point, *The Lord of the Rings* are novels in which the author creates a fully-imagined Secondary World, a world which Tolkien takes as seriously as Homer took the Trojan War, and a world in which the characters walk with destiny. The story of Frodo's attempt to return the One Ring to Mount Doom and destroy it is more than just the story of one Hobbit's quest: it is the account of a period of middle Earth's history during which an evil power was thwarted, and the true king returned to his throne, and the fate of the known world decided for generations to come. External indications of the seriousness with which Tolkien took his narratives include the appendices to *The Lord of the Rings* as well as the whole mythology behind it later published as *The Silmarillion*. As material published since his death has shown, there was a creation of even larger than epic proportions from which *The Lord of the Rings* sprang. In many ways, Middle Earth was his life's work.

The creation of Middle Earth certainly drew heavily on Tolkien's academic life. The names of the Dwarfs in *The Hobbit* and *The Lord of the Rings* come from the Norse Eddas as do the Trolls and the Elves. Gandalf's name, from the same source, can be translated as 'Sorcerer-Elf'.[33] Beorn, the shape-changer, is a character from Scandinavian legend. Smaug, the dragon, is very similar to the dragon in *Beowulf* – right down to knowing his treasure hoard so well that he can tell when a cup is missing. Aragorn and Galadriel come from Arthurian romance. As Gandalf becomes more of a guide and a wizard, he grows to resemble Merlin. The idea of Hobbits living in caves inside hills may have come from Tolkien's knowledge of the Celtic *sidhe* dwellers. Tolkien's style, too, comes from these traditional narratives; it is the plain and direct language of the Greek epics, the Norse sagas, the *Mabinogi*, and the *Song of Roland*, valuable especially for its clarity and its flexibility.[34]

Tolkien once intimated that *The Lord of the Rings* 'contains, in the way of presentation that I find most natural, much of what I have personally received from the study of things Celtic'.[35] That 'way of presentation' and the borrowings I have already cited (a few of the many) have, unfortunately, left Tolkien, and the other High Fantasy writers who draw on older materials, open to the charge of being derivative. Such a charge might be true if Tolkien, or any other High Fantasy author, were trying to write a modern novel, but such is not the case. I believe that Tolkien was trying to write, in so far as such might be possible in the twentieth century, a Heroic Age narrative, perhaps an epic; and in doing so, he was following in an ancient and honourable tradition.[36] As Gerhard Herm states in *The Celts*, one of the areas of learning which the druids were to master included 'all of the old stories circulating that the public invariably wished to hear again and again, in the same traditional form'.[37] The ancient tellers were valued less for their creation of new stories than for their ability to tell an old story well. And judged by his performance, Tolkien is a pre-eminent storyteller.

In addition to its subject matter and style, High Fantasy also derives much of its power from the older materials it incorporates. The characters and archetypes from myth, legend, and folktale resonate with a power of their own.[38] Tolkien, one example among many, uses Light to represent good and order and uses Dark to represent evil and chaos, and in doing so, he employs archetypes traceable to many ancient mythologies. But such materials must be used in ways consistent with their traditional intent or value. When the reader picks up an Arthurian fantasy, he or she has a number of expectations about what the narrative will contain. If the expectations are met, the whole narrative will be enhanced by the Arthurian inclusion; if the expectations are violated (should Arthur be cast as an evil character, for example), the reader may, reacting negatively to this use of the Arthurian materials, reject the whole book. The well-integrated narrative, then, has not only the power of the fantastic, but also the power of the traditional materials included therein.

The power of High Fantasy, Stephen Donaldson suggests, is the power to portray internal conflicts. 'Put simply, fantasy is a form of fiction in which the internal crises or conflicts or processes of the characters are dramatised as if they were external individuals or events.'[39] Ursula LeGuin says that fantasy 'is a journey into the subconscious mind, just as psychoanalysis is. Like psychoanalysis, it can be dangerous; and *it will change you*' (italics in original).[40] And Lloyd Alexander asserts, 'If the creator of fantasy has done his work well, we should be a little bit different at the end of the journey than we were at the beginning. Maybe just for the moment, maybe for a long while.'[41] While these statements are true of much fantasy, they are especially true of High Fantasy; and if we understand the darker aspects of our own personalities better after Frodo's confrontation with Gollum in *The Lord of the Rings* or Ged's integration of his conscious Self with his Shadow in *A Wizard of Earthsea*, it is the result of the writer's ability to create High Fantasy and High Fantasy's power to tell us something about ourselves.

* * *

Regarded thus, fantasy is certainly not an escape literature. As Alexander notes, these fantasies 'are written by adults living in an adult world, trying to cope with it and understand it, subjected to and responding to all the pressures and problems of real life. If the writer of fantasy is a serious creator, his work is going to reflect this'.[42] *The Lord of the Rings* may, indeed, have been influenced by Tolkien's experiences in World War I, however well he kept them hidden; and Grahame's *The Wind in the Willows* may, on one level, reflect a 'Victorian paranoia about the mob'. [43] If so, those novels are reflecting 'the pressures and problems' with which Tolkien and

Grahame had to deal. In this way, too, modern fantasy is a creation of the modern world.

NOTES

1. L. Carter, *Imaginary Worlds* (New York: Ballantine, 1973), p. 5.
2. K. Hume, *Fantasy and Mimesis* (New York: Methuen, 1984), p. 20.
3. K. Hume, *Fantasy and Mimesis*, p. 21.
4. C. S. Lewis, *An Experiment in Criticism* (Cambridge: Cambridge University Press, 1965), p. 50.
5. S. C. Fredericks, 'Problems of Fantasy', *Science Fiction Studies* 5 (March 1978), p. 37.
6. C. N. Manlove, *Modern Fantasy: Five Studies* (Cambridge: Cambridge University Press, 1975), p. 3.
7. E. Rabkin, *The Fantastic in Literature* (Princeton: Princeton University Press, 1976), p. 15.
8. G. K. Wolfe, 'The Encounter With Fantasy', in Roger C. Schlobin (ed.), *The Aesthetics of Fantasy Literature and Art* (Notre Dame: Notre Dame University Press, 1982), pp. 1–2.
9. J. R. R. Tolkien, 'On Fairy-Stories', in *The Tolkien Reader* (1947, New York: Ballantine, 1966), p. 37.
10. J. Yolen, *Touch Magic* (New York: Philomel, 1981), p. 77.
11. L. Alexander, 'Flat-Heeled Muse', *Hornbook* 41 (1965), pp. 141–6.
12. E. Cameron, *The Green and Burning Tree* (Boston: Little, Brown, 1962), p. 17.
13. B. Attebury, *The Fantasy Tradition in America from Irving to LeGuin* (Bloomington: Indiana University Press, 1980), p.2.
14. C. W. Sullivan III, *Welsh Celtic Myth in Modern Fantasy* (Westport: Greenwood Press, 1989), pp. 94–6.
15. B. Aldiss, *Billion Year Spree* (New York: Schocken Books, 1974), pp. 20–37.
16. S. Prickett, *Victorian Fantasy* (Hassocks: Harvester Press, 1979), p. 151.
17. H. Carpenter. *Secret Gardens* (Boston: Houghton Mifflin, 1985), p. 41.
18. S. Prickett, *Victorian Fantasy*, p. 156.
19. H. Carpenter, *Secret Gardens*, p. 37.
20. S. Prickett, *Victorian Fantasy*, p. 150–97.
21. H. Carpenter, *Secret Gardens*, p. 83.
22. L. Dégh, 'Folk Narrative', in R. Dorson (ed.), *Folklore and Folklife* (Chicago: University of Chicago Press, 1972), p. 63.
23. L. Carter, *Imaginary Worlds*, p. 25.
24. R. N. Lynn, *Fantasy Literature for Children and Young Adults: An Annotated Bibliography*, 3rd edn (New York: Bowker, 1989), p. 155.
25. Ibid.
26. G. K. Wolfe, *Critical Terms for Fantasy and Science Fiction* (Westport: Greenwood Press, 1986), p. 52.
27. D. Bisenieks, 'Tales from the "Perilous Realm": Good News for the Modern Child', *Christian Century* 91 (1974), p. 617.

28. U. K. LeGuin quoted in E. Cameron, 'High Fantasy: *A Wizard of Earthsea'*, *Hornbook* 47 (1971), p. 130.

29. U. K. LeGuin, 'From Elfland to Poughkeepsie', in S. Wood (ed.), *The Language of the Night* (New York: Berkley Books, 1982), p. 84.

30. U. K. LeGuin, 'From Elfland to Poughkeepsie', p. 85.

31. C. W. Sullivan III, *Welsh Celtic Myth in Modern Fantasy*, p. 106.

32. L. Alexander, 'Substance and Fantasy', *Library Journal* 91 (1966), p. 6158.

33. S. Sturluson, *The Prose Edda*, trans. J. Young (Berkeley: University of California Press, 1966), p. 41.

34. U. K. LeGuin, 'From Elfland to Poughkeepsie', p. 83.

35. J. R. R. Tolkien, 'English and Welsh', in *Angles and Britons* (Cardiff: University of Wales Press, 1963), p. 1.

36. C. W. Sullivan III, 'Name and Lineage Patterns: Aragorn and Beowulf', *Extrapolation* 25 (1984), pp. 244–5.

37. G. Herm, *The Celts* (New York: St. Martin's Press, 1976), p. 239.

38. K. Hume, *Fantasy and Mimesis*, p. 88.

39. S. Donaldson, *Epic Fantasy in the Modern World* (Kent: Kent State University Libraries, 1986), pp. 3–4.

40. U. K. LeGuin, 'From Elfland to Poughkeepsie', p. 84.

41. L. Alexander, 'Truth About Fantasy', *Top of the News* 24 (1968), p. 174.

42. L. Alexander, 'Truth About Fantasy', p. 170.

43. H. Brogan, 'Tolkien's Great War', in G. Avery and J. Briggs (eds), *Children and Their Books* (Oxford: Clarendon Press, 1989), p. 353; and N. Philip, '*The Wind in the Willows*: the Vitality of a Classic', in G. Avery and J. Briggs (eds), *Children and Their Books* (Oxford: Clarendon Press, 1989), p. 313.

8
Winnie-the-Pooh and Domestic Fantasy

PETER HUNT

Winnie-the-Pooh and *The House at Pooh Corner* are among the most famous and successful of children's books, but they are not generally regarded as being among the most famous and successful fantasies. Yet they are classic examples of the domestic fantasy, a genre that encapsulates the distinctive features of fantasy in general, and inter-relates the adult and children's forms of it.

Both books have been bestsellers since their publication; *Winnie-the-Pooh* had sold half a million copies in Britain by 1936, and when the New York publisher Dutton produced their new uniform edition in 1935, the two books had been through no less than 153 USA impressions between them. This popularity has continued; very many editions and variations are currently in print or on tape, from *The Pooh Cookbook* to the Latin translation *Winnie-ille-Pu*, and from the philosophical commentary *The Tao of Pooh*[1] and Frederick R. Crews's satire on literary critics, *The Pooh Perplex*, to the adaptations by the Walt Disney studios.

It is no accident that Milne's books have been as popular with adults as with children, because they are far from being 'pure' children's books; they have a decidedly double focus – and this double focus is important if we consider the books as fantasy.

The *Pooh* books are a remarkable publishing phenomenon; the more so in that the books are palpably of the 1920s, of the English middle-classes, and the work of a sophisticated novelist/playwright who had a very ambivalent attitude both to his own childhood and his son's childhood (as well as to the *Pooh* books). They have become part of British culture, in the sense that they are passed along from generation to generation almost as part of a secret code of language. But what makes them survive, apart from the massive inertia built into the children's book publishing establishment? Indeed, what makes them survive despite the fact that they encapsulate so many of the central dilemmas of children's books?

One answer, suggested by Alison Lurie, is that the books 'tell a story with universal appeal to anyone anywhere who finds himself, like most children, at a social disadvantage',[2] but I think there is far more to it than that. They satisfy both children's and adults' interpretations of fantasy (which, of course, overlap, as do children and adults), and – (as Sullivan has suggested) – fantasy puts its roots down into subconscious human universals, and thus can transcend its local surface features. If it has replaced the romance as the illegitimate twin of the novel, it has also replaced it as the 'adolescent' twin, the area where the imagination is liberated, rather than (as with the 'mature' novel), being at the service of the naturalistic and the solipsistic. As Ursula leGuin observed, many modern adults – or, at least, modern adult critics – are afraid of dragons.

Many of the key elements of fantasy are there in *Winnie-the-Pooh* and *The House at Pooh Corner* – security and (and from) adventure, the Secondary World, the heroic or controlling figure and the anti-hero (with both of whom the reader can identify), the alien race, anthropomorphism, team stereotypes – and sexism.[3] They may in some ways be adapted to a child view (as they are in those other ambiguous classics, the *Alice* books) but equally they are all central features of fantasy and are all centrally relevant to childhood. By cutting the usually larger-than-life elements of fantasy down to smaller-than-life animated toys, Milne preserved the power of fantasy and made it accessible to children.

As Eleanor Cameron observed of fantasy (she did not include *Winnie-the-Pooh* in her list), modern fantasy adds to the 'assaults' on the natural laws of the world

> the element of contrast which provide a kind of reverberation out of the fact that within the world of every day a little pool of magic exists possessing a strange, private, yet quite powerful and convincing reality of its own.[4]

That 'powerful and convincing reality' is, of course often a function of escape or wish-fulfilment – but if fantasy is wish-fulfilment, then just whose wishes are being fulfilled in the *Pooh* books? What is their significance in defining the relationship between fantasy and children's books?

Margery Fisher has observed that

> Children should always be able to enjoy the tales at the stage when they can imagine that toys are as real and as alive as the postman

and can retreat into the special, private world of wood and stream which Milne affectionately externalized from his own family experience.[5]

In a sense, this is a definition of childhood that has nothing to do with years passing.

In the fictionalised image of the forest around Cotchford Farm, shrunk from 500 to 100 acres,[6] the small adventures of Pooh and his friends and acquaintances are played out in the classic fantasy setting of a secure and *comprehensible* country. Here, nothing can *really* go wrong; from the point of view of the characters the worst that can happen is getting wet or temporarily running out of honey. The absence of any mundane considerations such as where the jars of honey come from may be a function of the middle-classness of the text – but it is also a function of fantasy, where such matters are generally unimportant.

The forest is a 'Secondary World', an 'enchanted place'; it is neither garden nor wild country, and its boundaries are vague; the focus is on the characters, and the setting is only a setting. E. H. Shepard's drawings, which many people (including Milne) have seen as an integral part of the text, do, however, give 'a local habitation'. His pictures of Sussex woodland and heathland are perhaps not as cosy and 'safe' as his illustrations of the Thames valley for *The Wind in the Willows*, but they are essentially English and of their time, rather than, as in true fantasy, remaining timeless. This 'localisation' is emphasised by the map endpapers that appear in some editions. Unless the map is integral to the story (as in *The Lord of the Rings*, but *not* as in *The Hobbit*) then it can be at best unnecessary, and at worst destructive (as in *The Wind in the Willows*). Curiously, then, the 'Secondary World' is in a sense threatened by one of its creators – and as much for the writer as the reader. The public certainly identified the books as much as Shepard's work as of Milne, a fact resented by the Milnes, both father and son.[7]

Even more curious is the fact that the element that *most* threatens that enchantment of the world of the *Pooh* books is the intrusive voice of the adult narrator. The fumbling and linguistically ambivalent opening of *Winnie-the-Pooh*, where Christopher Robin is both character and auditor, the equally painful 'Contradiction' (or Introduction) to *The House at Pooh Corner*, which begins by saying that the characters are now going to say goodbye, and the ending, where Christopher Robin prepares to grow up, are the points at which the fantasy world is most undermined. Many fantasies that are not totally set in the Secondary World begin by journeying to it by some magical incident (*The Lion, the Witch and the Wardrobe*), or natural phenomenon (*The Wizard of Oz*), or by establishing that it is dream (*Alice in Wonderland*), or some other psychological state (William Mayne's *A Game of Dark*), or by some narrative device. Mary Norton's *The Borrowers* has been rightly described as 'a model to tease the readers into fantasy'.[8] The fantasy world itself is then defined by the relationship with the 'real' world. Many fantasies derive much tension from whether the characters can make the return journey (some don't – as in E. Nesbit's *Harding's Luck* or David MacKee's *Not Now Bernard*), others from the ambiguity of the relationship (Allan Garner's *Elidor*); very few indeed appear to threaten the entire fantasy.

And this is what Milne comes perilously close to doing in his 'framing' of the *Pooh* stories. His two supposedly reassuring statements, which begin and end *The House at Pooh Corner* – 'the forest will always be there . . . and anybody who is Friendly with Bears can find it' (p. x)[9] and 'wherever they go, and whatever happens to them on the way, in that enchanted place on [*sic*] the top of the Forest, a little boy and his Bear will always be playing' (p. 178) seem to be necessary *because* Milne has framed the fantasy world so that it is two *unimportant* things – the ephemeral product of the father–son relationship – a game, and a rather patronisingly–played game, at that – and merely a place that Christopher Robin passes through on his way to somewhere else.

The evil genius in the world of Pooh is the authorial voice (if not the author himself), a fantastic creature who is rather difficult to circumvent. In a profound sense, Milne was breaking the fundamental laws of fantasy. As that notable fantasist George MacDonald put it, writing of 'The Fantastic Imagination', once an author has invented a world, 'the highest law that next comes into play is, that there shall be harmony between the laws by which the new world has begun to exist; and in the process of his creation, the inventor must hold by those laws. The moment he forgets one of them, he makes the story, by its own postulates, incredible'.[10] Milne said that when he had finished his four 'children's books' (his inverted commas), 'as far as I was concerned the mode was outmoded'.[11] It may well be that he never really adopted the mode at all. As in so many well-loved books (as, perhaps with many well-loved teddy-bears) the input from the reader or owner outweighs the dubious motives of the creator.

However, within the body of the text, within the unthreatened stories in the fantasy, there is security, and that security rests in a character who, in the real world, also had a highly ambivalent relationship with his fantasy self.

Thus, Pooh Bear is not alarmed by any noises outside in the forest at night.

> "What can it be?" he thought. "There are lots of noises in the Forest, but this is different one . . . it's a noise of some kind, made by a strange animal. And he's making it outside my door. So I shall get up and ask him not to do it." (*Pooh Corner*, pp. 19–20)

But this confidence is underpinned by the confidence Pooh has in the *other* figure that children can identify with. His first question to the ebullient Tigger is 'Does Christopher Robin know about you?' (*Pooh Corner*, p. 21) Christopher Robin, unlikely candidate as he is, is the adjudicator of this Secondary World, the Mage to whom the other characters turn, the Gandalf of the Hundred Acre Wood.

He lives in the 'Tardis'-like hollow tree, 'at the very top of the forest', where, however much it rains 'the water couldn't come up to *his* house'. (p. 135)[12] He is the only one who understands about Eeyore's tail; who would not let any harm come to Roo; who appears in almost every story, often as *deus ex machina*. As Rabbit says: 'What does Christopher Robin think about it all? That's the point.' (*Pooh Corner*, p. 105) There is no doubt that for many readers, he plays out the fantasy of control. This can either be seen – as it generally is – as a cosy and amiable relationship, by which, through Christopher Robin, the child-reader can relate to the animate toys, or – as Roger Sale points out – as something a little less lovable:

> The books are essentially about the fact that Christopher Robin is now too old to play with toy bears. His is given a world over which he has complete power and if he is not very attractive as a deus-ex-machina in story after story, if he is never as interesting as the Pooh and Piglet to whom he condescends, the pleasures of his power are clear enough.[13]

Perhaps most significantly for the downtrodden escapers who might be said to be the primary readers of fantasy (escaping for a moment, perhaps, from life, or the novel), is the presence of the ultimate anti-hero, Pooh bear – whose name, like the great fantasy (and folk) heroes is a matter of mystery. When Christopher Robin 'explains' the name to the narrator – an explanation that explains nothing – the narrator observes, 'I hope you [understand] because it is all the explanation you are going to get'. (*Winnie-the-Pooh*, p. 2). Pooh is both mystic and guizer; he wins by innocence and child-like qualities. Both adult and child reader can sympathise and empathise; Sam Gamgee is his first cousin. At his best, Pooh is both the inside and outside of childhood – especially in contrast with the vicissitudes of adulthood:

"Good morning, Eeyore." said Pooh.
"Good morning, Pooh Bear," said Eeyore gloomily, "If it *is* a good morning," he said. "Which I doubt." said he.
"Why, what's the matter?"
"Nothing, Pooh Bear, nothing. We can't all, and some of us don't. That's all there is to it."
... Pooh sat down on a large stone and tried to think this out. It sounded to him like a riddle, and he was never much good at riddles, being a Bear of Very Little Brain. So he sang *Cottleston Pie* instead. (*Winnie-the-Pooh*, pp. 71, 72)

None of the other characters share quite this mixture of bland insouciance and concern for others, but they do share their essential nature; as with other fantasy worlds, they are not quite of normal flesh – or normal stuffing – even if they are clearly related to familiar life-forms. As both stuffed toys and pseudo-animals, they can fall from trees, live on malt extract, or, in Eeyore's case, have a tail nailed back on – but once a natural law has been subverted everything continues logically – at least, as we have seen, well within the borders that Milne was inclined to subvert.

This is partly a function of animism. It is commonly held that children – and this is a defining characteristic of childhood – are more inclined to attribute human characteristics to inanimate objects.[14] (This is generally regarded as a social solecism in adulthood.) Yet here, because of the sentimental excuse – (which Milne himself would not have countenanced, at least intellectually) – the animate stuffed toys can relate both to adults and to children. What began as a private family joke becomes universal because of its extra-textual relevance. In fantasy, the things closest emotionally to the reader become animate. So it is, quintessentially, with *Winnie-the-Pooh* and *The House at Pooh Corner*. Margaret Blount sums this up:

Human is what the child wants his toy or pet to be, the substitute friend or brother, like himself *but exempt from all the dreary rules attached to childhood and growing up.* [My italics][15]

In fantasy, human is what the reader wants *everything* to become.

Alongside this reassuring, friendly, group-identification aspect of fantasy, many fantasies deal with some kind of alien race. The *Pooh* books take on what is for children the ultimate in alien races – the adults. Unlike most children's books, where the adults are 'outside' the texts, or distinctively of themselves, the adults in Milne's stories (ignoring the authorial characterisation) are of the same apparent species as the children. The conflict is internal. Thus we find Pooh (the bland, the confident, the mystic child), and his friend Piglet (the small, nervous, but very brave child), aided (slightly) by Tigger (the wild child) and Roo (the baby), pitted against a formidable array of adult traits. There is Rabbit (the egocentric, sarcastic boss), Owl (the pretentious and insecure egocentric adult), Eeyore (the depressive egocentric), and Kanga (the loving, but firm mother); each of them represent conflict of one kind or another, a way for the reader (the child) to fantasise superiority or victory in an alien world.

Griffith and Frey have suggested that the 'stories' humour comes from their pattern of concentric circles of knowingness'. They go on:

> the larger animals understand things that the smaller animals do not; Christopher Robin understands things that the larger animals do not; and the narrator and reader understand things that Christopher Robin does not. The tone is very comforting; miniature rivalries for respect and attention are ultimately resolved, in the assumption that everyone is to be loved despite his foibles and stupidities, or maybe even *because* of them.[16]

This is a very tempting thesis, but it ignores the fact that fantasy *is* uncomfortable, and *is* a displacement, even though a large majority of fantasies do – and this is one thing that links them with children's books in general – reach a resolution. (It might be argued that *The House at Pooh Corner* is an ambivalent text precisely because it does *not* reach a satisfactory resolution.) As Margaret Blount observed, 'The individuality of Pooh, Piglet, and friends is at times uncomfortably and sadly life-like',[17] and Roger Sale feels that the relationships are presented in terms of 'fradulent and shallow snobbery'.[18]

It is well known that the characterisations stemmed from the stuffed toys and Milne's wife's characterisations, but it is notable that the two most 'adultist', and perhaps least sympathetic characters did not: 'Only Rabbit and Owl,' Milne wrote, 'were my own unaided work,'[19] while Kanga (along with Tigger and Roo) were later toys, 'carefully chosen, not just for the delight that they might give to their new owner, but also for their literary possibilities'.[20] This somewhat calculating attitude, which does not relate very sympathetically to childhood, comes out in the behaviour of the characters.

Rabbit is the classic example; he is the character who brings rationality – and with it, fear – into the idyllic fantasy world. As we have seen, Pooh Bear is not in the least bit afraid of the noises in the night; the forest is a golden world. But when he visits Rabbit, Rabbit at first plays a pointless (and not child-like) game of using false voices, claiming that he didn't know that his visitor was Pooh. Pooh says,

> "Who did you think it was?"
> "Well, I wasn't sure. You know how it is in the Forest. One can't have *anybody* coming into one's house. One has to be *careful*."
> (*Winnie-the-Pooh*, p. 24)

Rabbit and Pooh are at opposite extremes. Pooh, counting his honey pots, is worried whether he has fourteen or fifteen. Rabbit says:

> "Does it matter?"
> "I just like to know," said Pooh humbly. "So as I can say to myself: 'I've got fourteen pots of honey left.' Or fifteen, as the case may be. It's sort of comforting."
> "Well, let's call it sixteen," said Rabbit. (*Pooh Corner*, pp. 36–7)

This is very much in the spirit of the 'jelly-bellied flag flapper' who addresses the boys' school in Kipling's *Stalky and Co*; the adult totally misunderstands the values of childhood. The difference is, perhaps, simply between the mystic Pooh to whom poetry comes sometimes, and Rabbit 'who never let things come to him, but always went and fetched them'. (*Pooh Corner*, p. 82) It is Rabbit, the slightly corrupt adult (in the rationalist mould of Boromir in *The Lord of the Rings*), who motivates two of the stories by wanting to get rid of, first, Tigger, and secondly, Kanga and Roo. He is basically, against change;

they do not fit into the established society: Tigger does not know the social rules, Kanga is a foreigner, and, what is worse, a female. While in a fantasy directed primarily at adults, Rabbit might have been bloodily defeated, the weapons that defeat him are more appropriate to childhood, and the private mystical power of childhood. When Rabbit gets them all lost in the fog (while the intended victim, Tigger the innocent, merely trots home) Pooh waits until Rabbit has lost himself thoroughly.

> "Now then, Piglet, let's go home."
> "But, Pooh," cried Piglet, all excited, "Do you know the way?"
> "No," said Pooh. "But there are twelve pots of honey in my cupboard, and they've been calling to me for hours. I couldn't hear them properly before, because Rabbit *would* talk . . ." (*Pooh Corner*, p. 123)

As Pooh reflects later, 'Rabbit's clever . . . I suppose . . . that's why he never understands anything." (p. 130)

Fortunately, as in much fantasy, the evil – or, at least, the less than pleasant – characters, cannot agree among themselves. Owl, that personification of a cliché, has problems concealing his ignorance from the insistent Rabbit ('Owl looked at him and wondered whether to push him off the tree . . .' [*Pooh Corner*, p. 79]; Kanga mistakes Owl's shawl for a 'dirty old dishcloth' (pp. 154–5); Eeyore is disgusted that writing is a thing that Rabbit knows (p. 89). This is writing on the child's side; the child's fantasy of incompetent adults who make mistakes. Unlike the *Alice* books, in which the adults are seen as inexplicably insane in one way or another, here they are generally rather pathetic creatures, seen through and gently patronised by turns by the child-characters and the child-readers.

Eeyore, that *miserimus* of children's literature, exemplifies this. In some ways, his attitudes may be mystifying to the child. As Nicholas Tucker has observed, 'although older children will understand the muddled, egocentric world of small children's thinking . . . they will miss a great deal of the more subtle adult humour . . .'[21] However, self-imposed though it is, Eeyore's misery (if not its inordinate continuance) is understandable, and Pooh and Piglet do treat him with some sympathy and respect. His automatic responses are generally ignored:

> "Hallo, Eeyore," they called out cheerfully.
> "Ah,' said Eeyore. "Lost your way?"

"We just came to see you," said Piglet. "And to see how your house was. Look, Pooh, it's still standing!" "I know," said Eeyore. "Very odd. Somebody ought to have come down and pushed it over." (*Pooh Corner*, p. 130)

Thus although the fantasy world does place adults and children on the same footing, the relationship remains ambivalent. This fantasy, like most others, does compensate for inadequacies in the actual world, but it is not an over-confident fantasy.

Within the child figures, from Pooh to Roo, there is a shifting hierarchy; each has his strengths at certain times. As *The Lord of the Rings* or *Watership Down* or the work of Enid Blyton or (less coherently) 'Carolyn Keene', and a thousand other fantasies (many produced in Hollywood and set in the Second World War) demonstrate, it is convenient to have a hierarchy of heroic and anti-heroic stereotypes.

Only rarely, in the *Pooh* books does this hierarchy reflect the outside world in a way that is naturalistic, rather than threatening, and, significantly, the most obvious case is in the mother-child rela tionship of Kanga and Roo. Much of this is a simple reflection of normality:

"We'll see," said Kanga, and Roo, who knew what *that* meant, went into a corner, and practised jumping out at himself, partly because he wanted to practise this, and partly because he didn't want Christopher Robin and Tigger to think that he minded when they went off without him. (*Pooh Corner*, pp. 121–2)

Piglet, similarly, is well aware of being small and weak ('I thought Tiggers were smaller than that' [*Pooh Corner*, p. 24]), but has his own fantasies (fantasies on top of fantasies, as it were) of, for example, heroically dealing with the Heffalump.

And, finally there is an element in the fantasy of the *Pooh* books which they share with many fantasies – and not only fantasies of the same period: sexism. This, of course marks both the date of composition and the social background of the *Pooh* books, just as it does in *The Wind in the Willows* or Tolkien's *oeuvre*, but it is also, through stereotyping, very typical of many contemporary fantasies – they are *male* fantasies. It may seem unlikely, but Milne is in a tradition (perhaps most obviously exemplified by Kenneth Grahame) that excludes, and probably fears, the female.

122 *Peter Hunt*

For adult readers, there is one extra dimension in the books, that of nostalgia. Milne 'delivers a golden world'; this is a pastoral, partly delivered by the prose, but, as we have seen, more by Shepard's drawings. The occasional verbal scene-setting has a hint of reaching back to a lost utopia, as, perhaps, every generation does.

> By the time it came to the edge of the Forest the stream had grown up, so that it was almost a river, and, being grown-up, it did not run and jump and sparkle along as it used to do when it was younger, but moved more slowly . . . There was a broad track, almost as broad as the road, leading from the Outland to the Forest, but before it could come to the Forest, it had to cross this river. (*Pooh Corner*, p. 91)

The convention of the inside and the outside worlds is clear enough, and although the sentimentality may militate against the books for the adult reader in the 1990s, it is not clear that it would have done so in earlier decades, or does so now for the child-reader.

This discussion has been primarily about the relationship of the text and the reader; but fantasy can be very therapeutic for the author; can we learn anything from the relationship between Milne and his text, if such a thing is reachable? Milne's own childhood, and the childhood of his son, were both estranged from their parents;[22] it may well be that Milne was exorcising his relationship problems, as well as writing an idyll at a time when he was psychologically troubled by the memory of war. It is possible to sense the fumblings of the narrative voice, the occasional intrusions of the storytelling-situation as ways in which the isolated author was trying to make a link with child and text that he wished were there.

To the purist critic (or, at least, anyone brought up in the major Anglo-American critical traditions of the last sixty-odd years) such speculations are illegitimate. Yet they form part of the total meaning of the text for all but the least-informed reader. The line between adult/child and reality/fantasy is a fine one; can an adult, reading the *Pooh* books, forget that Brian Jones, the 1960s guitarist with The Rolling Stones was drowned in the swimming-pool at Cotchford? Can they forget, for that matter, that people write critical articles about the books, perhaps just as fantastic, if less tragic, a happening.

However, this whole thesis may seem to be a reductive, 'adultist' approach, putting too much weight onto the shoulders of the 'Bear of Very Little Brain' – especially post-Crews. As Carpenter and

Prichard have observed, any subsequent critic risks 'sounding like one of Crews' parodies – and also [of] saying rather less'. Yet, they conclude:

But, *pace* Crews, it remains to be said that Milne's characters are archetypal and the books' incidents endlessly useful as metaphors for daily life.[23]

But if children's books represent, at their best, a mediation between the adult- and the child-world, then they also mediate between fantasy as understood by, and appropriate to, the child and fantasy as understood by, and appropriate to, the adult. In either case, the *Pooh* books are not simply parochial, flawed, egocentric texts; they are central to any discussion of literary fantasy, and the need it fulfils in child, adult, and author.

NOTES

1. Katie Stewart, *The Pooh Cook Book*, (London: Methuen, 1971); Benjamin Hoff, *The Tao of Pooh*, London: Methuen, 1982; Frederick R. Crews, *The Pooh Perplex*, (New York: Dutton, 1965).
2. Alison Lurie, *Don't Tell the Grown Ups*, (Boston: Little, Brown, 1990), p. 145.
3. See Sullivan, above; and Rosemary Jackson, *Fantasy: the literature of subversion*, (London: Methuen, 1981).
4. Eleanor Cameron, *The Green and Burning Tree*, (Boston: Little, Brown, 1969), pp. 16–17.
5. Margery Fisher, *Classics for Children and Young People*, (South Woodchester: Thimble Press, 1986), p. 9.
6. See Christopher Milne, *The Enchanted Places*, (London: Eyre Methuen, 1974).
7. See Gillian Avery, 'The Cult of Peter Pan', *Word and Image* 2, 2, April–June, 1986, p. 177; Rawle Knox (ed.), *The Work of E. H. Shepard*, (London: Methuen, 1979), pp. 112–13. I am most indebted to Kerry Wilson, *From Tenniel To Shepard* (Unpublished M. Phil. dissertation, University of Kent, 1990) for these references.
8. Sam Leaton Sebasta and William J. Iverson, *Literature for Thursday's Child*, (Chicago: Science Research Associates, 1975), p. 179.
9. A. A. Milne, *The House of Pooh Corner*, (New York: Dutton, new edition, 1935).
10. George MacDonald, *A Dish of Orts*, (London: Newnes, 1905), p. 314.
11. A. A. Milne, *It's Too Late Now* (London: Methuen, 1939), p. 242.
12. A. A. Milne, *Winnie-the-Pooh* (New York, Dutton, new edition, 1935).

124   *Peter Hunt*

13.   Roger Sale, *Fairy Tales and After*, (Cambridge, Mass.: Harvard University Press, 1978), p. 17.
14.   See Peter Hunt, *Criticism, Theory, and Children's Literature*, (Oxford: Blackwell, 1991), pp. 57–60; Bruno Bettelheim, *The Uses of Enchantment*, (New York: Knopf, 1976), pp. 45–7.
15.   Margaret Blount, *Animal Land*, (New York: Morrow, 1974), p. 170.
16.   John W. Griffith and Charles H. Frey (eds), *Classics of Children's Literature*, (New York: Macmillan, 1981), p. 939.
17.   Margaret Blount, *Animal Land*, p. 180.
18.   Roger Sale, *Fairy Tales and After*, p. 16.
19.   A. A. Milne, *It's Too Late Now*, p. 239.
20.   Quoted by Humphrey Carpenter and Mari Prichard, *The Oxford Companion to Children's Literature*, (Oxford: Oxford University Press, 1984), p. 576.
21.   Nicholas Tucker, *The Child and the Book*, (Cambridge: Cambridge University Press, 1981), p. 98.
22.   See A. A. Milne, *It's Too Late Now*, and Christopher Milne, *The Enchanted Places*.
23.   Humphrey Carpenter and Marie Prichard, *The Oxford Companion to Children's Literature*, p. 576.

9
The Dorothys of Oz: A Heroine's Unmaking

MARK I. WEST

Many nineteenth-century Americans wrote fantasy stories for children, but it was not until the publication of L. Frank Baum's *The Wonderful Wizard of Oz* in 1900 that America produced a fantasy story that rivalled Lewis Carroll's 1865 classic, *Alice's Adventures in Wonderland*.[1] Consequently, historians of children's literature tend to focus on Baum's pioneering work in the area of fantasy. Baum's pioneering spirit, however, can also be seen in his portrayal of girls, especially Dorothy Gale, the most famous of his girl characters. In a time when children's authors seldom allowed their girl characters to venture far from home, let alone go off on adventures, Baum sent Dorothy on a bona fide quest.

Dorothy is one of the very first girl characters in American or British children's literature to experience the type of heroic quest that Joseph Campbell analysed in his seminal study, *The Hero with a Thousand Faces*. As outlined in Campbell's book, heroic quests tend to follow a basic pattern: 'A hero ventures forth from the world of common day into a region of supernatural wonder: fabulous forces are there encountered and a decisive victory is won: the hero comes back from this mysterious adventure with the power to bestow boons on his fellow man.'[2] Dorothy's adventure closely parallels Campbell's synopsis of the heroic quest. The only significant difference is that Dorothy does not 'bestow boons' when she returns to Kansas at the end of the book, but the reason she does not is simply that the book ends before she has a chance to do much of anything but greet her Aunt Em. In subsequent Oz books, such as *The Lost Princess of Oz*, Dorothy often uses her power and knowledge to help others.

Throughout the entire Oz series, Dorothy never loses her heroic qualities, but in the famous 1939 MGM film *The Wizard of Oz*, Baum's heroic Dorothy was transformed into a much weaker and meeker character. This transformation was not the result of a sexist plot. In

125

Aljean Harmetz's *The Making of "The Wizard of Oz"*, Harmetz explained that Noel Langley, Florence Ryerson, Edgar Allan Woolf, and the numerous other screenwriters who helped turn Baum's *The Wonderful Wizard of Oz* into the screenplay gave very little thought to Dorothy's character. They deviated from Baum's book mainly because they wanted to create a more fully developed frame story and sought to tighten up what they saw as Baum's rambling plot.[3] In the process, however, they changed or removed most of the scenes in which Baum's Dorothy behaves heroically and made her conform to stereotypical notions of femininity.

The book begins in a rather straightforward manner. Dorothy, the dog Toto, Aunt Em, and Uncle Henry are briefly introduced, a few words are said about Kansas, and then their farm is hit by a cyclone. The movie, however, begins with an elaborate frame story. The script writers created this frame story in order to establish connections between Dorothy's situation in Kansas and her experiences in Oz. Although the frame story cleverly foreshadows several aspects of Dorothy's adventures in Oz, it also serves to undermine Dorothy's heroic potential. The script writers introduced three farm hands who are later transformed into the Scarecrow, the Tin Woodman, and the Cowardly Lion. The farm hands are adults, and they tend to be protective of Dorothy. Because this pattern is established in the opening scenes of the movie, the script writers naturally assumed that the pattern would persist when Dorothy meets the somewhat altered versions of these characters in Oz.

In both the book and the movie, a cyclone transports Dorothy and Toto to Oz, but the events leading up to this scene differ significantly in the two versions of the story. Baum's Dorothy has the option of going down into the cellar before the cyclone hits the house, but she decides not to seek safety until she rescues Toto. She is in the process of taking Toto to the cellar when the cyclone tears the house off its foundation and sends it hurtling toward Oz. By risking her life in order to save Toto, Dorothy shows that she has the makings of hero within her. The script writers' Dorothy does nothing heroic before going to Oz. In the movie, she is returning home, after having briefly run away, when the cyclone hits. A piece of flying debris strikes her on the head and knocks her unconscious. She then dreams about being swept off to Oz. In this version, Dorothy is not risking her life to save Toto; she is simply in the wrong place at the wrong time. Moreover, her trip to Oz does not really seem like the beginning of a quest because it is reduced to being a dream.

From the point when Dorothy's house lands on top of the wicked Witch of the East to the point when Dorothy and her three compatriots enter the Emerald City, the book and the movie are quite similar. There are, however, some subtle differences in the two portrayals of Dorothy's relationship with her fellow travellers. In the book, Dorothy functions as the leader of the group. They all depend on one another, but Dorothy is the one who generally speaks for the group and who makes most of the major decisions. In the movie, Dorothy's travelling companions seem more like her guardians than her followers. When the Witch of the West threatens the group, for example, the Scarecrow tells Dorothy, 'I'm not afraid of her! I'll see you get safely to the Wizard now.' The Tin Woodman then chimes in, 'I'll see you reach the Wizard, whether I get a heart or not!'[4]

The two versions of the story diverge at the point when Dorothy and her companions first meet the Wizard of Oz. Baum's Dorothy enters the Throne Room by herself and asks the Wizard to send her back to Kansas. He tells her that before he will grant her wish, she must first 'kill the wicked Witch of the West'.[5] The Dorothy in the movie enters the Throne Room in the company of her companions. After Dorothy and the other characters make their various requests, the Wizard tells them that they must first bring him 'the broomstick of the Witch of the West'.[6] On the surface, the two versions of this scene seem quite similar, but in terms of Dorothy's character, there are significant differences. By singling out Dorothy and requiring her to kill the Witch, Baum's version puts Dorothy in much the same position of a medieval knight who is being sent forth to slay a dragon. In the script writers' version, Dorothy is not actually required to kill the Witch, nor is the responsibility of defeating the Witch assigned primarily to her. While this version is a bit less daunting, it lessens the likelihood that Dorothy will emerge from the mission as a hero.

What happens to Dorothy and her companions after they set out to defeat the Witch differs widely from one version of the story to the other. In the book, Dorothy, Toto, and the Cowardly Lion are captured and brought to the Witch's castle while the Scarecrow and the Tin Woodman are seemingly destroyed and left for dead in the woods outside the castle. The Witch of the West imprisons the Lion and enslaves Dorothy. In addition to forcing Dorothy to perform various onerous chores, the Witch constantly tries to gain possession of Dorothy's magical shoes. Dorothy, however, refuses to comply with the Witch's demands. At one point, the Witch manages to snatch one of the shoes, and this causes Dorothy to rebel. She picks up a bucket of water and angrily throws it at the Witch, causing the Witch to melt and die.

In the movie, only Dorothy and Toto are captured and brought to the Witch. Shortly after Dorothy and Toto arrive at the castle, the Witch grabs Toto and threatens to drown him unless Dorothy gives her the magic slippers. Dorothy readily agrees to this deal, but when the Witch tries to take off the slippers, she receives a powerful shock. The Witch then says that the only way she can get the slippers is by killing Dorothy first, and she starts making plans to do so. At this point, Toto escapes and runs into the woods, where he finds the Scarecrow, the Tin Woodman, and the Cowardly Lion. These characters then set out to rescue Dorothy. Eventually they find Dorothy locked up in a little room in the castle. They break her out of the room and are in the process of sneaking out of the castle when the Witch discovers them. The Witch vows to destroy all these characters one by one, starting with the Scarecrow. She sets the Scarecrow on fire, but Dorothy puts out the fire by pouring the bucket of water on the Scarecrow. Some of the water, however, splashes onto the Witch, and the Witch then melts.

Dorothy kills the Witch in both versions, but in Baum's version Dorothy comes across as a much more forceful and heroic character. Baum's Dorothy never gives in to the Witch's demands, whereas the script writers' Dorothy does. Baum's Dorothy defeats the Witch without anyone's help, whereas the script writers' Dorothy waits for male rescuers to save her. Perhaps the most important difference is that Baum's Dorothy is confrontational in her dealings with the Witch. In Baum's version, Dorothy deliberately throws the water on the Witch. Even though Dorothy does not know that this action will kill the Witch, it is still an aggressive act. The Dorothy in the film never confronts the Witch. The script writers' Dorothy kills the Witch, but she does so in a completely unaggressive way. Thus, Baum's Dorothy emerges from her confrontation with the Witch as a victor, whereas the script writers' Dorothy continues to see herself as a helpless little girl.

The differences between the two Dorothys become especially evident in the stories' conclusions. Immediately after killing the Witch, Baum's Dorothy frees the Cowardly Lion and rescues the Scarecrow and the Tin Woodman. They all then make their way back to the Emerald City where they discover that the Wizard does not have the power to send Dorothy back to Kansas. Dorothy learns that the only person in Oz who can help her is Glinda, the Witch of the South. Dorothy therefore leads her companions on a journey south, and after several adventures they meet Glinda. Glinda tells Dorothy that the magical shoes that Dorothy has been wearing can take her home. All she needs to do is 'knock the heels together three times and command the shoes to carry' (p. 257) her back to Kansas. After saying her goodbye, Dorothy follows Glinda's instructions, and an instant later she is running into Aunt Em's arms.

Unlike the book, the movie ends soon after Dorothy accidentally splashes water on the Witch. As soon as the Witch is pronounced dead and Dorothy is given the Witch's broomstick, the movie jumps to the scene in which Dorothy and her companions present the broomstick to the Wizard. They soon learn that the Wizard is a humbug, and Dorothy is about to give up hope of returning to Kansas when Glinda suddenly appears. Glinda tells Dorothy that she had 'always had the power to go back to Kansas', but she could not use this power until she had learned a certain lesson. Dorothy is then asked what she has learned from her experiences in Oz, and Dorothy answers, 'I think that it wasn't enough just to want to see Uncle Henry and Auntie Em. It's that if I ever go looking for my heart's desire again, I won't look any further than my own backyard' (p. 128). Glinda nods approvingly and instructs Dorothy to click her heels together and think to herself, 'There's no place like home' (p. 129). Dorothy then wakes up from her dream. The movie concludes with Dorothy exclaiming, 'I'm not going to leave here ever, ever again, because I love you! And, oh, Auntie Em, there's no place like home!' (p. 132).

Dorothy's identity formation process figures prominently in both endings, but the end results are far different. For Baum's Dorothy, her victory over the Witch proves to be a key turning point. Not only does she seem to have more confidence after this event, but she also becomes a stronger leader. A sign of this change is her determination to rescue the Scarecrow and the Tin Woodman. Her concern for the welfare of others is also evident when she is explaining to Glinda why she wants to return to Kansas. Instead of talking about being homesick, she says, 'My greatest wish now is to get back to Kansas, for Aunt Em will surely think something dreadful has happened to me, and that will make her put on mourning' (p. 254). Baum's Dorothy returns to Kansas a maturer and more confident girl for having been to Oz.

The Dorothy in the movie never becomes a leader or achieves a sense of self-reliance. What she carries away from her experiences in Oz is a sense of being chastened for having run away and a determination not to go on any more adventures. Her pledge never to look beyond her 'backyard' when searching for her 'heart's desire' is similar to Peter Pan's pledge never to grow up. Both pledges indicate a fear of change. Although the pledge that Dorothy makes in the movie does not preclude her from growing up, it places severe restrictions on her future adult roles. Thus, in contrast to Baum's Dorothy, the script writers' Dorothy embraces the sexist notion that girls should not aspire to a life beyond the home.

The differences between the two Dorothys reflect broader conflicts concerning the role of females in society. In creating Dorothy, Baum knowingly went against prevailing notions of femininity. Unlike many men from this period, Baum disagreed with the limitations that society then placed on females. He came to this position in part because of his close associations with the women's suffrage movement. His mother-in-law, Matilda Joslyn Gage, was one of the leading woman's rights advocates of the time. She lived with Baum and his family for many years, and she encouraged Baum to question societal assumptions about gender roles.[6]

This questioning spirit can be seen in many of Baum's books for children. In *The Wonderful Wizard of Oz*, he introduced a strong female protagonist. In some of his other children's books, he explored such topics as androgeny and matriarchal societies. He even wrote a number of books under various female pseudonyms, including Edith Van Dyne and Laura Bancroft. In other words, Baum's decision to send Dorothy on a quest was not an isolated experiment but was instead an outgrowth of his questioning attitude toward societal gender roles. Like some other fantasy authors, Baum used his fiction to explore alternatives to the status quo. By creating a less sexist society, he gave his readers a chance to look at their own society from another perspective.

In contrast to Baum, the script writers were not especially interested in imagining alternative societies or criticising the status quo. They contributed to the script not because they admired Baum's book or shared his views but simply because the movie's producer assigned them to the project. These writers were all under contract with MGM, and they worked on whatever scripts MGM's producers sent their way. In this case, the producer charged them with task of transforming Baum's story into a movie that would have mass appeal. These writers often disagreed over particular aspects of the movie's plot, but they all worked under the assumption that the script should reflect the values and attitudes that were prevalent in American society at that time. For this reason, they automatically made Dorothy and the other characters in the movie behave in accordance with traditional gender roles. Ironically, the script writers' portrayal of Dorothy seems outdated and sexist by contemporary standards while Baum's Dorothy comes across as a heroine whose time has nearly arrived.

NOTES

1. For more information about fantasy stories written by Americans during the nineteenth century, see M. I. West (ed.), *Before Oz: Juvenile Fantasy Stories from Nineteenth-Century America* (Hamden, Conn.: Archon Books, 1989).
2. J. Campbell, *The Hero with a Thousand Faces* (Princeton, New Jersey: Princeton University Press, 1949), p. 30.
3. A. Harmetz, *The Making of "The Wizard of Oz"* (New York: Knopf, 1977), pp. 25–59.
4. M. P. Hearn (ed.), *The Wizard of Oz: The Screenplay* (New York: Delta, 1989), p. 76.
5. L. F. Baum, *The Wonderful Wizard of Oz* (New York: Morrow, 1987), p. 128.
6. M. P. Hearn (ed.), *The Annotated Wizard of Oz* (New York: Clarkson N . Potter, 1973), p. 14. See also G. De Luca and R. Natov, 'Researching Oz: An interview with Michael Patrick Hearn', *Lion and the Unicorn*, vol. 11, no. 2 (1987), p. 55.

Further Reading: A Select List

The place of publication is London unless stated otherwise.

CRITICAL AND HISTORICAL APPROACHES TO CHILDREN'S LITERATURE

Avery, G., *Childhood's Pattern: A Study of the Heroes and Heroines of Children's Fiction, 1770–1950*, Hodder and Stoughton, 1975.

___, *Nineteenth Century Children: Heroes and Heroines in English Children's Stories 1780–1900*, Hodder and Stoughton, 1965.

Bratton, J. S., *The Impact of Victorian Children's Fiction*, Croom Helm, 1981.

Butts, Dennis (ed.), *Good Writers for Young Readers*, Hart-Davis, 1977.

Carpenter, H., *Secret Gardens: A Study of the Golden Age of Children's Literature*, Allen & Unwin, 1985.

Chambers, N. (ed.), *The Signal Approach to Children's Books: A Collection*, Kestrel, 1980.

Harvey Darton, F. J., *Children's Books in England: Five Centuries of Social Life*, 3rd edition revised by Brian Alderson, Cambridge: CUP, 1982.

Dixon, Bob, *Catching Them Young*, vol. 1, 'Sex, Race and Class in Children's Fiction', Pluto, 1977.

Harrison, B.T., 'Literature for Children: a Radical Genre', *The New Pelican Guide to English Literature*, vol. 8, Harmondsworth: Penguin, 1983.

Hawes, Joseph M., and Hiner, N. Ray (eds), *American Childhood: A Research Guide and Historical Handbook*, Westport, Conn.: Greenwood, 1985.

Hazard, Paul, *Books Children and Men*, translated by M. Mitchell, Boston: The Horn Book, 1972.

Hunt, Peter, *Children's Literature: The Development of Criticism*, Routledge, 1990.

Inglis, Fred, *The Promise of Happiness: Value and Meaning in Children's Fiction*, Cambridge: CUP, 1981.

Hollindale, Peter, 'Ideology and the Children's Book', *Signal*, no. 55, Gloucester: Thimble Press, 1988, pp. 3–22.

Jordan, Alice M., *From Rollo to Tom Sawyer and Other Papers*, Boston: The Horn Book, 1948.

Keenan, Hugh T. (ed.), 'Narrative Theory and Children's Literature,' *Studies in the Literary Imagination*, vol. XVIII, Atlanta: Georgia State University, 1985.

Leeson, Robert, *Children's Books and Class Society: Past and Present* Writers and Readers Publishing, 1977.

___, *Reading and Righting: The Past, Present and future of Fiction for the Young*, Collins, 1985.

Pawling, Christopher,'*Watership Down*: Rolling Back the 1960s', in C. Pawling (ed.) *Popular Fiction and Social Change*, Macmillan, 1984.

Meigs, Cornelia (ed.), *A Critical History of Children's Literature: A Survey of Children's Books in English from Earliest Times to the Present*, New York: Macmillan, 1964.

Pickering, Samuel Jr, *John Locke and Children's Books in Eighteenth Century England*, Knoxville: University of Tennessee Press, 1981.

Propp, V., *Morphology of the Folk Tale*, 1st edition translated by L. Scott and with introduction by S. Pirkova-Johnson, 2nd revised edition, L. A. Wagner with new introduction by A. Dundas Austin: University of Texas, 1975.

Rose, Jacqueline, *The Case of Peter Pan or the Impossibility of Children's Literature*, Macmillan, 1984.

Salway, Lance (ed.), *A Peculiar Gift: Nineteenth Century Writings on Books for Children*, Kestrel, 1976.

Smith, Joseph H. and Kerrigan, William, *Opening Texts: Psychoanalysis and the Culture of the Child*, Baltimore: Johns Hopkins University Press, 1985.

Townsend, John Rowe, *Written for Children: An Outline of English-Language Children's Literature*, 3rd revised edition, Harmondsworth: Penguin, 1987.

GENRES

The Adventure Story

Campbell, Joseph, *The Hero with a Thousand Faces*, Bollingen Series XVII, New Jersey: Princeton University Press, 1971.

Dunae, Patrick, 'British Juvenile Literature in an Age of Empire, 1880–1914,' an unpublished PhD thesis, University of Manchester, 1975.

Fisher, M., *The Bright Face of Danger: An Exploration of the Adventure Story*, Hodder & Stoughton, 1986.

Green, Martin, *Dreams of Adventure, Deeds of Empire*, Routledge & Kegan Paul, 1980.

Howarth, Patrick, *Play Up and Play the Game: The Heroes of Popular Fiction*, Eyre Methuen, 1973.

Lofts, W. O. G., and Adley, D. J., *The Men Behind Boys' Fiction*, Howard Baker, 1970.

Richards, Jeffrey (ed.), *Imperialism and Juvenile Literature*, Manchester: Manchester University Press, 1989.

Sandison, A., *The Wheel of Empire: A Study of the Imperial Idea in Some Late Nineteenth and Early Twentieth Century Fiction*, Macmillan, 1967.

Turner, E. S., *Boys Will Be Boys: The Story of Sweeney Todd, Deadwood Dick, Sexton Blake, Billy Bunter, Dick Barton et al.*, Michael Joseph, 1975.

Fantasy

Bettelheim, Bruno, *The Uses of Enchantment: The Meaning and Importance of Fairy Tales*, Thames & Hudson, 1976.

Blount, Margaret, *Animal Land: The Creatures of Children's Fiction*, Hutchinson, 1974.

Jackson, Rosemary, *Fantasy: The Literature of Subversion*, Methuen, 1981.

Lynn, Ruth Nadelman, *Fantasy for Children and Young Adults: An Annotated Bibliography*, 3rd edition, New York: Bowker, 1989.

Manlove, C. N., *Modern Fantasy: Five Studies*, Cambridge: CUP, 1975.

Prickett, S., *Victorian Fantasy* Brighton: Harvester, 1979.

Sewell, Elizabeth, *The Field of Nonsense*, Chatto & Windus, 1952.

Swinfen, Ann, *In Defense of Fantasy: A Study of the Genre in English and American Literature since 1945*, Routledge & Kegan Paul, 1984.

Tolkien, J. R. R., *Tree and Leaf*, Allen & Unwin, 1964.

Zipes, Jack, *Fairy Tales and the Art of Subversion: the Classical Genre for Children and the Process of Civilization*, Heinemann, 1983.

___, *Victorian Fairy Tales: The Revolt of the Fairies and Elves*, Methuen, 1987.

The Family Story

Coveney, Peter, *The Image of Childhood: The Individual and Society. A Study of a Theme in English Literature*, Harmondsworth: Penguin, 1967.

Gorham, Deborah, *The Victorian Girl and the Feminine Ideal*, Croom Helm, 1982.

Grylls, David, *Guardians and Angels: Parents and Children in Nineteenth-Century Literature*, Faber & Faber, 1978.

Lasch, Christopher, *Haven in a Heartless World: The Family Besieged*, New York: Basic Books, 1977.

Laski, Marghanita, *Mrs. Ewing Mrs. Molesworth and Mrs. Hodgson Burnett*, Arthur Barker, 1950.

Macleod, Anne Scott, *A Moral Tale: Children's Fiction and American Culture 1820–1860*, Hamden, Conn.: Archon, 1973.

Meigs, Cornelia, *Louisa M. Alcott and the American Family Story*, Bodley Head, 1970.

Stone, Lawrence, *The Family, Sex and Marriage in England 1500–1800*, Weidenfeld & Nicolson, 1977.

Strickland, Charles, *Victorian Domesticity: Families in the Life and Art of Louisa M. Alcott*, Alabama: University of Alabama Press, 1985.

The School Story

Brazil, Angela, *My Own Schooldays*, Blackie, 1926.

Cadogan, Mary, and Craig, Patricia, *You're a Brick, Angela! The Girls' Story 1839–1985*, Gollancz, 1986.

Lofts, W. O. G., and Adley, D. J., *The World of Frank Richards*, Howard Baker, 1975.

Mangan, J. A., *Athleticism in the Victorian and Edwardian Public School* Cambridge: CUP, 1981.

Orwell, George, 'Boys's Weeklies,' *Critical Essays*, Secker & Warburg, 1946.

Quigly, Isabel, *The Heirs of Tom Brown: The English School Story*, Chatto & Windus, 1982.

Richard, Jeffrey, *Happiest Days: The Public Schools in English Fiction*, Manchester: Manchester University Press, 1988.

Wakeford, John, *The Cloistered Elite: a Sociological Analysis of the English Public Schools*, Macmillan, 1969.

Warner, Philip, *The Best of British Pluck: The Boy's Own Paper*, MacDonald & Jane's, 1976.

Index